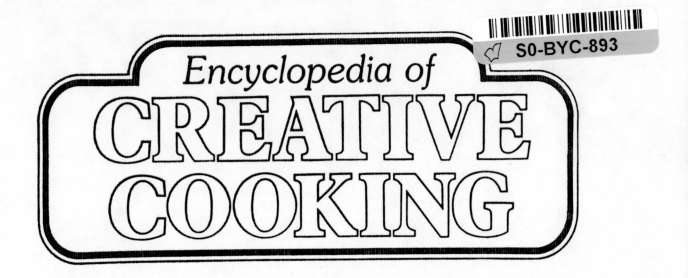

Encyclopedia of
CREATIVE
COOKING

Volume 12
Party Menus

Editors for U.S. editions
Steve Sherman and Julia Older

ECB Enterprises Inc.

Entertaining:
Dinner Party Menus

*Midsummer
Dinner*

Creamy Fish Pots

★

Beef en Croûte

★

Green Salad

★

**Tangerine Sherry
Cake**

Creamy Fish Pots

 ★

2 tablespoons mixed butter and oil
1 shallot, minced
⅔ cup water
⅔ cup dry white wine
juice 1 lemon
salt and pepper
¾ lb. haddock, cut into ½-inch
  cubes
1 tablespoon butter
1 tablespoon flour
⅔ cup mayonnaise
¼ lb. cooked jumbo shrimp, peeled,
  deveined and chopped
6 unpeeled cooked jumbo shrimp
6 slices lemon
6 slices cucumber

1 Heat the butter and oil in a pan. Sauté the shallot for 1 minute. Add the water, wine, lemon juice, and seasoning and boil gently for 10 minutes.

2 Add the haddock. Cover and cook gently for 15-20 minutes. Mix the butter and flour and whisk it into the pan. Bring the mixture to a boil, stirring ocassionally. Boil for 2 minutes and cool.

3 Blend in the mayonnaise and chopped shrimp. Divide the sauce among 6 individual casseroles.

4 Decorate each casserole with an unpeeled shrimp and lemon and cucumber twists.

Serves 6

Tip: You can, of course, use any white fish in this recipe, instead of haddock. If you feel extravagant, add some chopped lobster tails.

Beef en Croûte

 ★

1 tablespoon oil
3 lb. rolled rib roast
2 tablespoons butter
1 onion, chopped
¼ lb. mushrooms, finely
  chopped
2 tablespoons chopped parsley
salt and pepper
10 ozs. puff pastry
few sprigs watercress

1 Preheat the oven to 400°F. Heat the oil in a large pan and sear the meat quickly on all sides to seal the juices. Transfer both the oil and meat to a roasting pan and roast for 45 minutes. Cool.

2 Melt the butter in a pan and sauté the onion for 5 minutes until soft. Add the mushrooms, parsley and seasoning. Cover and sauté for 5 more minutes.

3 Roll out the pastry to a rectangle large enough to completely cover the meat. Spread ⅓ of the stuffing over the center of the pastry and place the meat on top. Spread the rest of the stuffing over the meat. Dampen the edges of the pastry and fold them up over the meat like a parcel. Trim.

4 Place the meat, seam downward, in a roasting pan. Roll out the pastry trimmings and cut them into 'leaves' to decorate the top. Brush the top with a little milk. Increase the oven temperature to 425°F. and cook the beef for 40-45 minutes until the pastry is crisp and golden.

5 Transfer the meat to a serving dish and garnish with watercress.

Serves 6-8

Tangerine Sherry Cake

  ★

2¾ cups all-purpose flour
1¼ cups warm milk
1 tablespoon dry yeast
2 tablespoons sugar
2 eggs, beaten
¼ cup softened butter
¾ cup sugar
1¼ cups water
2 tablespoons sherry
6 fresh tangerines, peeled and
  sectioned
1¼ cups heavy cream, whipped

1 In a bowl, mix ½ cup of the flour with the milk. Sprinkle on the yeast and leave until frothy. Add the sugar, eggs, butter and remaining flour and beat for 3 minutes. Turn the mixture into a buttered and lined 8-inch cake pan. Cover with a damp cloth and leave until the mixture rises almost to the top of the pan.

2 Preheat the oven to 400°F. Remove the cloth and bake the cake for 30-35 minutes. Cool on a rack.

3 Dissolve the sugar in the water over low heat and boil for 2 minutes. Remove from the heat and stir in the sherry. Reserve 2 tablespoons of the syrup and pour the rest over the cake. Let soak.

4 Split the cake in two. Arrange half of the tangerine sections over the bottom layer and spread with ⅔ of the cream. Cover with the top layer of cake. Arrange the rest of the tangerines in the center and brush them with the reserved syrup. Pipe whirls of the remaining cream around the rim and serve.

Serves 6-8

Creamy Fish Pots, Beef en Croûte and Tangerine Sherry Cake all taste delicious and together add up to a memorable meal

Autumn Feast

Scallops in Saffron Sauce

★

Cornish Hens Vigneronne

★

Herby Potato Bake

★

Avocado Whip

Scallops in Saffron Sauce

12 scallops
2 shallots, minced
1¼ cups white wine
juice 1 lemon
sprig thyme
pinch saffron
salt and pepper
¼ cup heavy cream
16 whole cooked, peeled, deveined
  shrimp

1 Place the scallops, shallot, wine, lemon juice, thyme and saffron in a pan and cook gently for 5-6 minutes.

2 Remove the thyme and strain the liquid into another pan. Season and boil for 5 minutes. Stir in the cream and simmer for 4 minutes.

3 Arrange the scallops on a serving dish and pour on the sauce. Decorate with the cooked shrimp and serve.

Serves 4

Tip: When you serve this dish as an appetizer, you can allow three scallops per person. However, you can also serve it as an attractive main course. If so, allow six to eight scallops per person, and serve each portion on a bed of plain, boiled rice.

Cornish Hens Vigneronne

4 Cornish hens
salt and pepper
2 tablespoons butter
2 tablespoons oil
½ lb. pearl onions
1 small shallot, chopped
2 teaspoons tomato paste
⅔ cup grape juice
½ chicken bouillon cube, crumbled
1 bay leaf
½ lb. green grapes, halved

For the Stuffing:
¼ lb. sausage meat
1 egg yolk
1 teaspoon chopped parsley

1 Mix the stuffing ingredients together and stuff and truss each hen. Season.

2 Preheat the oven to 400°F. Heat the butter and oil and brown the hens. Transfer to an ovenproof dish. Brown the onions in the same fat and add. Cover and roast for 20 minutes.

3 When the hens are cooked, drain off the fat into a small pan. Keep the hens and onions warm. Sauté the shallot, then add the tomato paste, grape juice, bouillon cube and bay leaf. Boil for 10 minutes, strain and season.

4 Arrange the grapes around the hens and serve with the gravy.

Serves 4

Herby Potato Bake

 ★

6 medium-size potatoes, peeled
  and thinly sliced
1 clove garlic, crushed
⅔ cup light cream
2 teaspoons chopped chervil
pinch nutmeg
salt and pepper
1 shallot, finely grated
1 cup grated cheese

1 Preheat the oven to 350°F. Par-

boil the potatoes in a pan of boiling water for 4-5 minutes and drain.

2 Mix together the garlic, cream, chervil, nutmeg, seasoning and grated shallot.

3 Alternate the potato and cheese layers in a buttered dish, reserving a little cheese. Pour in the cream mixture and sprinkle with the remaining cheese.

4 Bake for about 45 minutes until cooked and golden brown.

Serves 4

Avocado Whip

2 avocados
1 tablespoon lemon juice
⅔ cup heavy cream
2 tablespoons light cream
2 tablespoons sugar
1 teaspoon grated lemon rind
few drops pistachio extract
2 egg whites

1 Peel the avocados and remove the seeds. Mash the pulp and mix in the lemon juice.

2 Whip the creams until thick. Add the sugar, grated lemon rind and pistachio flavoring. Fold into the mashed avocado mixture.

3 Beat the egg whites until they are stiff and glossy. Fold into the avocado mixture and mix well.

4 Spoon the mixture into individual serving dishes and chill in the refrigerator for at least 1 hour. Serve plain, or decorated with whipped cream and chopped nuts.

Serves 4

Hens Vigneronne, garnished with grapes and pearl onions, is wonderful for serving at special dinner parties

Grape
Drink
Made from Grape juices from more than
Made in England by HP Bulmer

Look 'n Cook Avocado Whip

1 The ingredients for the avocado whip: light cream, heavy cream, sugar, lemon, eggs, 2 avocados, pistachio flavoring **2** Peel the avocados with a potato peeler. Remove the seeds and mash the pulp with a fork. Add the lemon juice **3** Whip the creams until stiff **4** Fold the sugar, grated lemon rind and a few drops of pistachio flavoring into the whipped cream **5** Fold the flavored cream into the mashed avocado mixture

6 Beat the egg whites until stiff and glossy, then fold into the avocado mixture **7** Blend well together **8** Divide the avocado whip among 4 individual serving dishes and chill in the refrigerator for at least 1 hour before serving. You can decorate this dish with cream and chopped nuts

Italian Spread

Mussels Anacapri

★

Veal Venezia

★

Duchesse Potatoes

★

Broccoli

★

Strawberry Meringue

Mussels Anacapri

32 mussels, washed and scraped
2 cloves garlic, crushed
2 onions, chopped
1¼ cups dry white wine
sprig thyme
salt and pepper
2 tablespoons chopped parsley
2 tablespoons butter
2 tablespoons flour
3 egg yolks, beaten
juice ½ lemon

1 Place the mussels, garlic, onion, wine, thyme, seasoning and parsley in a large pan and bring to a boil. Boil for 5-6 minutes until the mussels open. Discard any mussels which remain closed.

2 Strain off the liquid into another pan. Break off and throw away one side of each hinged mussel shell. Arrange the mussels in an oven-proof dish and keep warm.

3 Melt the butter in another pan and stir in the flour. Cook for 1 minute, without browning, then add the reserved mussel liquid. Bring to a boil, stirring all the time.

4 Gradually mix the sauce into the beaten egg yolks. When well blended, return to the pan and bring back to a boil. Add the lemon juice and check the seasoning. Pour

Mussels Anacapri are served in a delicious wine-flavored sauce and are a typically Italian way to start a formal meal

the sauce over the mussels and serve.

Serves 4

Veal Venezia

four ¼-lb. veal cutlets
2 tablespoons flour
¼ lb. butter
2 cloves garlic, crushed
1 small shallot, chopped
⅔ cup sweet vermouth
2 tablespoons tomato paste
2 tomatoes, skinned, seeded and chopped
salt and pepper
pinch oregano
¼ lb. mushrooms, sliced

1 Beat the cutlets until flat. Sprinkle them with flour.

2 Heat ¼ cup butter in a skillet and gently sauté the veal until golden brown. Remove and keep warm.

3 Sauté the garlic and shallot for 2-3 minutes, then add the vermouth, tomato paste and chopped tomato. Season with salt and pepper and sprinkle in the oregano. Bring to a boil, stirring well, then simmer for about 10 minutes.

4 Heat the remaining butter in another pan and sauté the mushrooms until golden.

5 Arrange the cutlets in a serving dish and pour on the sauce. Garnish with the mushrooms. Serve with fresh broccoli and Duchesse potatoes.

Serves 4

Tip: You can also make this dish with red wine or Italian fortified wine, Marsala. Marsala will make the sauce sweeter in flavor and darker in color. For a more attractive appearance, sprinkle the finished dish with chopped fresh parsley.

Veal Venezia has a garnish of Duchesse potatoes and sauteed mushrooms, and evokes the flavors of Italian cuisine

For the Caramel:
20 sugar cubes
1 tablespoon water

1 Preheat the oven to 250°F. Place the egg whites in a mixing bowl and beat well until stiff and glossy. It will save time and energy if you use an electric beater.

2 Gradually add the sugar, 1 tablespoon at a time, beating well after each addition. When all the sugar has been added, the meringue should be very stiff.

3 Blend in the vanilla and fill a decorator's bag with the meringue mixture.

4 Pipe a circle of meringue, 7 inches in diameter, onto a sheet of wax paper. Pipe the remaining meringue into seven individual blocks, each 3 inches long and 1½ inches wide.

5 Place the meringue on a baking sheet and bake in the oven for about 2 hours. Remove when dried out but not colored. If the meringue starts to color, open the oven door for awhile.

6 Make the caramel: place the sugar and water in a saucepan and boil until you have a toffee-like sticky consistency.

7 Place the cooled meringue base on a serving plate. Arrange the meringue blocks around the sides to form a border, laying them on their sides. Stick them together with the caramel and place them in position.

8 Wash and hull the strawberries. Whip the cream until thick and stiff and flavor it with the Marsala. Fill a decorator's bag with the cream and pipe some across the base. Pile the strawberries up on top and pipe a large swirl of cream in the center, surrounded by smaller rosettes. Pipe a small swirl of cream between each of the meringue blocks on the edge of the plate. Decorate with the candied violets and serve.

Serves 4

Strawberry Meringue

  ★

Strawberry Meringue, decorated generously with swirls of whipped cream and violets, is a perfect dessert for summer

4 egg whites
1 cup sugar
2-3 drops vanilla extract
1 lb. strawberries

1¼ cups heavy cream
2 tablespoons Marsala
7 candied violets

Fillets of Sole with Grapes

8 fillets of sole
5 tablespoons butter
1 onion, chopped
bouquet garni
1⅔ cups court bouillon
salt and pepper
½ lb. seedless grapes
2 tablespoons apple brandy
2 shallots, chopped

1 tablespoon flour
½ cup white wine
⅔ cup light cream

1 Roll up the fillets and secure them with toothpicks. Melt 1 tablespoon of the butter in a large skillet. Sauté the onion until soft and add the bouquet garni, court bouillon and finally the fish. Season, cover and simmer for 15-20 minutes.

2 Mix the grapes and apple brandy and marinate for 15 minutes. Transfer the fish to a warm serving dish and keep warm. Reserve 1 cup of the court bouillon.

3 In a clean pan, melt the remaining butter and gently sauté the shallots. Stir in the flour and white wine and gradually add the reserved court bouillon. Season. Simmer gently for 5 minutes. Stir in the cream and grapes, pour over the fish and serve.

Serves 6–8

*Fillets of Sole with Grapes are
served in a rich cream sauce and
garnished with shrimp and grapes*

Brochettes of Pork
with Rosemary

1½ lbs. lean pork from the shoulder
  or loin
1 tablespoon fresh rosemary,
  minced
salt and pepper
¼ cup olive oil
few sprigs fresh rosemary

1 Cut the pork into 1-inch cubes and thread on 4 skewers. Blend the rosemary, seasoning and oil. Marinate the brochettes in the oil overnight.

2 Remove them from the marinade and broil, turning occasionally, for 10-15 minutes or until tender. Baste occasionally with a little oil from the marinade.

3 Arrange on a dish and decorate with a few rosemary sprigs.

Serves 4

Apricot Compote

2 lbs. fresh apricots
½ cup sugar
1 tablespoon sliced almonds

1 Halve the apricots and remove their seeds. Place them in a large saucepan with just enough water to half-cover them and sprinkle with the sugar. Cook gently for 5-10 minutes, watching to make sure that they do not dissolve into a purée. Transfer the apricots to a serving dish.

2 Boil the remaining syrup until it is thick and pour it over the apricots. Sprinkle with the flaked almonds and chill in the refrigerator. Serve with a bowl of whipped cream.

Serves 4–6

*Brochettes of Pork with Rosemary
are large meaty chunks of pork
flavored with aromatic sprigs of
fresh rosemary*

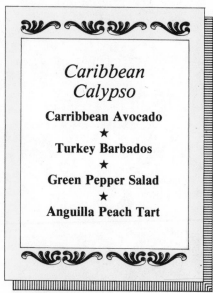

Caribbean Calypso

Carribbean Avocado

★

Turkey Barbados

★

Green Pepper Salad

★

Anguilla Peach Tart

Caribbean Avocado

2 ripe avocados
3 tablespoons oil
1½ tablespoons lemon juice
salt and pepper
1 teaspoon brown sugar
1½ tablespoons rum

1 Split the avocados lengthwise and remove the seeds. Blend the oil, lemon juice, seasoning and sugar together and pour a little over each avocado.

2 Chill in the refrigerator and, just before serving, arrange each avocado half on a lettuce leaf, sprinkle on a little rum and garnish with a twist of lemon.

Serves 4

Turkey Barbados

¼ cup flour
1 teaspoon ground ginger
1 teaspoon curry powder
four ½-lb. turkey cutlets
6 tablespoons butter
¼ cup rum
⅔ cup shredded coconut
3 tablespoons pineapple juice
⅓ cup stock
¼ cup heavy cream
salt and pepper
few sprigs parsley
6-8 slices pineapple

Anguilla Peach Tart is the perfect summer dessert with overlapping juicy peaches in a sticky apricot glaze

1 Mix together the flour, ginger and curry powder and use to coat the turkey cutlets. Heat the butter and fry the turkey until golden. Add the rum and ignite it. When the flames die down, remove the cutlets.

2 Add the coconut to the pan and brown quickly. Then stir in the pineapple juice and stock. Boil for 5 minutes, reduce the heat and stir in the cream and seasoning.

3 Arrange the turkey in a serving dish and cover with the sauce. Garnish with the parsley and pineapple and surround with boiled rice.

Serves 4

Anguilla Peach Tart

one 8-inch pie crust
5-6 peaches
2 tablespoons sugar
¼ cup apricot jam
1 tablespoon water
1 teaspoon lemon juice

1 Preheat the oven to 350°F. Line an 8-inch tart ring with the pastry and prick the base.

2 Scald the peaches in boiling water for a few seconds. Skin the peaches and remove the pits. Slice peaches thinly and overlap them in the crust. Sprinkle with sugar and bake for 25 minutes.

3 Heat the apricot jam, water and lemon juice in a small pan. Bring to a boil, simmer for 5 minutes, then strain and boil again. Brush the peaches and serve cold with cream.

Serves 4

Turkey Barbados has a spicy and exotic flavor — serve with plain, boiled rice and a sliced pepper salad

Chinese Banquet

Pork Spareribs
★
Oriental Fish Kebabs
★
Sweet and Sour Duck
★
Asparagus Salad
★
Fried Egg Noodles
★
Peking Apple
Fritters

Pork Spareribs

6 lbs. pork spareribs, cut into
  separate ribs
salt
$\frac{1}{3}$ cup honey
3 tablespoons soy sauce
1 tablespoon lemon juice
$\frac{1}{2}$ teaspoon ground ginger
few pineapple chunks

1 Preheat the oven to 375°F. Place the ribs in a roasting pan. Sprinkle with salt and bake for 45 minutes, pouring off the fat as it collects.

2 Meanwhile, gently heat the honey in a small saucepan. Stir in the soy sauce, lemon juice and ginger. Remove from the heat.

3 After 45 minutes, lower the oven temperature to 325°F. Pour the honey sauce over the ribs and cook 30 minutes more, turning the ribs occasionally. Decorate with the pineapple chunks and serve.

Serves 6

Oriental Fish Kebabs

$\frac{1}{2}$ lb. flounder fillets or any white
  fish

6 pieces gingerroot
$\frac{1}{4}$ lb. cooked shrimp, peeled and
  deveined
1 tablespoon melted butter

For the Marinade:
2 tablespoons honey
2 tablespoons oil

1 Mix the honey and oil. Place the fish in a non-metallic container, pour on the honey and oil and marinate for 1 hour.

2 Drain and dry the fish and cut it into strips. Cut the ginger into small pieces. Alternately thread the shrimps, fish and ginger onto 6 skewers. Brush them with the melted butter and cook them under a moderately hot broiler for 6-10 minutes or until the fish flakes easily. Turn the kebabs occasionally while they cook.

Serves 6

Sweet and Sour Duck

one 5-lb. duck
1 cup honey
1 tablespoon soy sauce
1 tablespoon sherry

1 Preheat the oven to 425°F.

2 Prick the duck all over with a carving fork and rub well with salt. Place the duck on a rack in a roasting pan on the middle shelf of the oven. Roast it for 30 minutes.

3 Reduce the heat to 375°F. and turn the duck. Mix the honey, soy sauce and sherry, and spread some over the duck. Continue roasting for 2$\frac{1}{2}$ hours, turning the duck frequently and basting with the rest of the sauce.

4 Transfer the duck to a serving dish. Surround it with deep-fried Chinese egg noodles, pineapple rings and a few sprigs of parsley. Garnish with a few pineapple pieces and serve.

Serves 6

Asparagus Salad

1$\frac{1}{2}$ lbs. asparagus
3 tablespoons soy sauce
1$\frac{1}{2}$ teaspoons sugar
$\frac{1}{2}$ teaspoon sesame oil

1 Trim the asparagus and cut it in 3-inch pieces. Parboil the tender tops for 30 seconds and the stems for 2 minutes. Drain.

2 Mix the soy sauce, sugar and oil and pour it over the asparagus. Chill in the refrigerator and serve.

Serves 6

Peking Apple Fritters

4 firm apples
1 egg
1 egg white
2 tablespoons flour
2 tablespoons cornstarch
oil for deep frying
$\frac{1}{4}$ cup oil
$\frac{3}{4}$ cup sugar
4 teaspoons white sesame seeds

1 Peel, core and cut each apple into quarters. Beat the egg and egg white until well blended and mix in the flour and cornstarch.

2 Heat the oil for deep frying to 375°F. Dip the apple wedges in the egg batter and fry them in the oil until golden brown. Remove and drain.

3 Place the oil and sugar in a saucepan. Heat gently, stirring constantly, until the sugar dissolves. Increase the heat and cook until the sugar begins to caramelize. Place the fritters on a serving dish and pour on the caramel sauce. Sprinkle with the sesame seeds and serve immediately.

Serves 6

*Peking Apple Fritters are encased
in a crisp batter and served in a
delicious caramel sauce with
sesame seeds*

Mediterranean Fare

**Mint and Cucumber
Fish Salad**

★

Veal Marsala

★

Sautéed Potatoes

★

Zabaglione *or*
Apricot Ice Cream

Mint and Cucumber Fish Salad

1 tablespoon butter
1 small onion, chopped
⅔ cup dry white wine
salt and pepper
½ lb. white fish fillets
½ small cucumber
2 teaspoons chopped mint
juice 1 lemon
12 cooked, peeled, deveined
   shrimp

1 Melt the butter in a skillet and sauté the chopped onion until soft. Add the white wine and seasoning and bring to a boil. Add the fish fillets, and reduce the heat to a gentle simmer. Cover and cook for 10 minutes. Remove from the heat and let the fish cool in the pan.

2 Scoop the seeds from the cucumber and cut it into small ¼-inch cubes.

3 When the fish has cooled, remove it from the pan and drain on absorbent paper. Flake it into small pieces and place them in a bowl with the cucumber and chopped mint. Sprinkle with the lemon juice, toss and chill for 30 minutes.

4 Just before serving, spoon the fish salad into 4 large scallop shells. Garnish each one with 3 shrimp and serve with lemon wedges and a

Mint and Cucumber Fish Salad is a tasty and refreshing start to a summer dinner party

bowl of mayonnaise.

Serves 4

Veal Marsala

4 veal cutlets
¼ cup flour
½ teaspoon mace
pinch paprika
pinch basil
pinch oregano
salt and black pepper
2 tablespoons oil
¼ cup butter
⅔ cup Marsala
⅔ cup heavy cream
juice ½ lemon
1½ cups mushrooms
2 teaspoons chopped parsley

1 Beat each veal cutlet with a meat mallet, flattening it to the largest possible size. Cut each piece in half.

2 Sift the flour onto a plate. Add the mace with the remaining spices, herbs and seasoning to the flour.

1 Place the egg yolks and sugar in a bowl and beat until light and fluffy.

2 Place the bowl over a saucepan of gently boiling water. Gradually add the brandy and Marsala, beating continuously, until the mixture thickens and becomes frothy.

3 Pour the Zabaglione into 4 glasses and serve immediately with lady fingers.

Serves 4

Apricot Ice Cream

¼ **cup dried apricots**
1 tablespoon brandy
⅔ **cup heavy cream**
½ **teaspoon grated lemon rind**
2 egg yolks, beaten
3 tablespoons confectioners' sugar

1 Place the apricots in a bowl and just cover them with boiling water. Leave for 1 hour. Drain and place them in a saucepan with fresh water. Simmer for 40-50 minutes or until they are soft. Pour off the water and work the apricots through a food mill, or purée them in a blender.

2 Place the puréed apricots in a bowl and stir in the brandy.

3 Place the cream, lemon rind and beaten egg yolks in a bowl over a saucepan of hot water and stir until a thick soft custard is formed. Remove from the heat and stir frequently to prevent a skin from forming until the custard begins to cool.

4 Stir in the confectioners' sugar and chill the custard thoroughly before straining it into the apricot purée. Blend well and transfer the mixture to an ice cream freezer or refrigerator tray. Freeze, stirring the mixture lightly 2 or 3 times. Serve in tall glasses.

Serves 4

---

3 Coat each cutlet with the seasoned flour and shake off any excess. Heat the oil and butter in a large skillet. When it is sizzling hot, add the cutlets and fry for 1½ minutes on each side, or until golden. Drain off the excess butter and oil.

4 Stir the Marsala into the pan and boil for 2 minutes. Stir in the cream and lemon juice and boil for 1 minute, stirring.

5 Transfer the cutlets to serving plates. Add the mushrooms to the sauce in the pan. Simmer, stirring continually, for 2 more minutes and pour the sauce over the cutlets. Garnish the cutlets with a little chopped parsley and

Veal Marsala is served with an attractive garnish of vegetables and makes a tasty dish for a formal dinner

serve with roasted new potatoes, and buttered asparagus and celery.

Serves 4

Zabaglione

6 egg yolks
½ **cup sugar**
¼ **cup brandy**
¼ **cup Marsala**

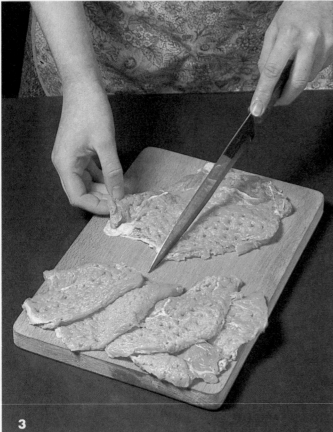

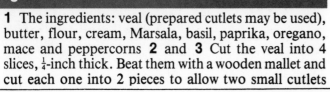

1 The ingredients: veal (prepared cutlets may be used), butter, flour, cream, Marsala, basil, paprika, oregano, mace and peppercorns **2** and **3** Cut the veal into 4 slices, ¼-inch thick. Beat them with a wooden mallet and cut each one into 2 pieces to allow two small cutlets per serving **4** Crush the mace with a pestle (or use ground mace) and add it to the sifted flour with the remaining spices, herbs and seasonings **5** Coat each cutlet with the seasoned flour and shake off any excess **6** Heat the butter and oil in a skillet until sizzling

hot. Add the cutlets and sauté them gently for 1½ minutes on each side. Drain off the surplus butter and oil **7** Stir the Marsala into the pan and boil gently for 2 minutes **8** Stir in the cream and lemon juice and boil for 1 more minute, while rotating and shaking the pan.

Place the cutlets on individual serving plates. Add the mushrooms to the pan and simmer them in the sauce for 1 minute. Pour the sauce over the cutlets and serve with new potatoes, asparagus spears and celery

Scottish Feast

Smoked Herring

★

Highland Hens

★

Orange Syllabub

★

Oaty Shortbread
Biscuits

★

Celtic Coffee

Smoked Herring

8 small smoked herring fillets
1¼ cups milk
1 small onion, sliced
salt and pepper
1 bay leaf
1 sprig mint
2 tablespoons butter
¼ cup flour
1 tablespoon whisky
½ teaspoon prepared mustard
juice ½ lemon
pinch grated nutmeg
2 teaspoons horseradish
1 tablespoon chopped parsley

1 Place the fillets in a small pan and cover with the milk. Add the onion, seasoning, bay leaf and mint, and poach gently for 15 minutes. Strain, reserving the liquid.

2 Make a roux with the butter and flour and cook for 1 minute. Add the strained fish liquid, a little at a time. Stir and bring to a boil. Season and add the whisky, mustard, lemon juice, nutmeg and horseradish. Cook gently for 5 minutes.

3 Arrange the fish fillets on a serving dish or in individual ramekins and pour on the sauce. Sprinkle with the chopped parsley and serve.

Serves 4

Highland Hens

2 Cornish hens, trussed and oven-ready
salt and pepper
2 slices bacon
¼ cup butter
1 cup cranberries
⅔ cup water
1 tablespoon honey
juice ½ lemon
few sprigs watercress

For the Sauce:
2 tablespoons oil
1 onion, chopped
1 carrot, chopped
1 branch celery, chopped
2 tablespoons flour
1 tablespoon tomato paste
1¼ cups water
½ beef bouillon cube
salt and pepper
pinch ground mace
3 tablespoons red port wine

1 Preheat the oven to 400°F. Season the hens with salt and pepper and wrap each one in a bacon slice. Tie the bacon in place with string, and place in a roasting dish. Dot the butter on the top. Roast in the oven for about 25 minutes until crisp and cooked, basting with the butter from time to time. Place the hens on a serving dish and keep warm.

2 Meanwhile, prepare the sauce. Heat the oil and sauté the vegetables until soft. Add the flour and cook for 1 minute, then stir in the tomato paste and water. Crumble in the bouillon cube, and season with the salt and pepper and mace. Bring the sauce to a boil, then simmer for 15-20 minutes. Strain and stir in the port wine. Return the strained sauce to the pan and heat through gently.

3 Place the cranberries, water, honey and lemon juice in a pan. Bring to a boil, then simmer until tender — be careful not to overcook them.

4 Cut the hens in half and serve the four portions on an attractive serving dish, garnished with the cranberries. Pour on a little of the sauce

and decorate with a few sprigs of watercress. Serve the rest of the sauce separately.

Serves 4

Orange Syllabub

2 oranges
3 tablespoons chopped dried apricots
¼ cup orange liqueur
⅓ cup sugar
1¼ cups heavy cream
2 tablespoons grated orange rind

1 Thinly peel the rind of 1 orange and place with the apricots in a small bowl. Cover with the squeezed juice of the 2 oranges and the liqueur. Marinate overnight.

2 Next day, remove the orange rind and apricots and stir in the sugar. Slowly stir in the cream and then beat until the syllabub stands in soft peaks.

3 Divide the reserved chopped apricots between 4 tall glasses and spoon in the syllabub. Sprinkle a little grated orange rind over the top of each one and serve with Oaty Shortcake Biscuits.

Serves 4

Tip: You can vary the flavor of this delicious dessert by experimenting with different spirits and liqueurs. Try Scotch whisky or the more traditional choice — an orange liqueur such as Cointreau.

Oaty Shortbread Biscuits

¼ lb. butter
1⅓ cups oats
¼ cup brown sugar

⅔ cup whole wheat flour
¼ teaspoon baking soda
pinch salt

1 Preheat the oven to 325°F. Heat the butter in a saucepan and, when melted, stir in the oats, sugar, flour, baking soda and salt.

2 Grease a shallow 6 × 9 cake pan and pour in the shortbread mixture. Spread the mixture evenly in the pan, pressing down the surface with a knife.

3 Bake in the preheated oven for 20-30 minutes. Run a sharp knife around the sides of the pan and cut the cooked shortbread while it is still hot into squares or fingers.

When cool, serve with the Orange Syllabub.

Makes about 18

Tip: Remember to press down firmly on the uncooked shortbread mixture with a knife blade. This will help to prevent the shortbread biscuits from crumbling when you cut them. Of course, you can serve these biscuits any time with coffee, cocoa, or tea.

Highland Hens are served in a wine flavored sauce and garnished with cranberries to make a tasty main course

Celtic Coffee

3 cups strong black coffee, freshly brewed
¼ cup sugar
⅔ cup Scotch whisky
⅔ cup heavy cream, whipped

1 Rinse out 4 coffee glasses with hot, not boiling, water. Pour in the coffee until each glass is about ¾ full.

2 Stir in the sugar and the whisky. Top with whipped cream.

Serves 4

1077

Seafood Special

Seafood Appetizer

★

Lobster Gratinée

★

Tomato and Basil Salad

★

Toledo Figs

Seafood Appetizer

1 pint mussels, cooked and shelled
¼ lb. cooked, peeled, deveined shrimp
½ cup mayonnaise
2 teaspoons lemon juice
salt and pepper
1 head lettuce, washed and shredded
18 whole cooked jumbo shrimp

1 Mix the shellfish, mayonnaise, lemon juice and seasoning.

2 Arrange in 6 individual glasses on the shredded lettuce.

3 Decorate each glass with 3 whole shrimp, a twist of lemon and a sprig of parsley.

Serves 6

Lobster Gratinée

three 1½-lb. lobsters, cooked
¼ cup oil
1 small onion, chopped
1 cup diced mushrooms
¼ cup fennel, chopped
¼ cup celery, chopped
2 cups breadcrumbs
1 cup white wine
1⅔ cups white sauce
1 hard-boiled egg, chopped
1 teaspoon prepared mustard
⅔ cup anise liqueur

Seafood Appetizer, with its attractive garnish of shrimp, parsley sprigs and lemon, tastes delicious

salt and pepper
juice 2 lemons
1½ cups grated cheese
1 tablespoon chopped parsley

1 Run the point of a sharp knife along the groove which runs across the lobster between the base of the head and the top of the tail. Then draw the knife through the groove running along the tail piece. Separate the two tail pieces as illustrated opposite. Remove and slice the meat and clean the shells.

2 Heat the oil and sauté the chopped vegetables until soft. Add the breadcrumbs and wine and bring to a boil. Stir in the white sauce and the chopped egg, mustard and anise liqueur. Cook gently for 5 minutes, season and add the crayfish meat. Heat through before dividing the mixture between the shells.

3 Sprinkle with lemon juice and grated cheese. Place under a hot broiler until golden brown. Sprinkle with chopped parsley, and garnish with parsley sprigs and lemon slices.

Serves 6

Toledo Figs

18 fresh or canned figs
½ cup brandy
½ cup sherry
½ teaspoon cinnamon
grated rind 1 orange
a little confectioners' sugar

1 Place the figs in a bowl and cover with the brandy, sherry, cinnamon and orange rind. Sweeten to taste with the sugar. Marinate for 1-2 hours.

2 Serve with whipped cream and chopped nuts.

Serves 6

Lobster Gratinée tastes as good as its flamboyant appearance suggests. Its tasty sauce is topped with cheese

Spanish Fiesta

Gazpacho

★

**Beef Loin Stuffed
with Mushrooms**

★

**Potatoes in Green
Sauce**

★

**Seville Orange
Cream**

Gazpacho

1 large tomato, skinned
1 small cucumber, skinned
1 green pepper, seeded
½ cup olive oil
¼ cup vinegar
salt and pepper
1 clove garlic, crushed
3 shallots, thinly sliced
6⅓ cups chicken consommé
croûtons to garnish

1 Seed the tomato and cucumber and cut them into ¼-inch cubes. Cut the green pepper into ¼-inch cubes.

2 Make a dressing by blending together the oil, vinegar, seasoning and garlic. Place all the vegetables in a bowl and pour on the dressing. Allow to stand for 1 hour, stirring occasionally.

3 Strain the vegetables and place them in a serving bowl. Pour on the consommé and chill in the refrigerator. Serve with toasted croûtons.

Serves 6

Tip: This light, cool and refreshing soup from the Andalusian region of Spain is perfect on a summer day and it can be varied in many ways. Try adding a few chopped black olives to the soup or replace a little of the chicken stock with chilled dry white wine and add a few ice cubes just before serving.

Beef Loin Stuffed with Mushrooms

2 lb. beef loin
2¼ cups dry white wine
¼ lb. butter
1 bay leaf
sprig thyme
1 onion, chopped
½ lb. mushrooms
salt and pepper
1 teaspoon chopped parsley

Gazpacho is a traditional soup from Spain—serve it ice cold with a garnish of toasted croûtons of white bread

1 Marinate the loin in the white wine overnight. Drain the loin, reserving the marinade, and dry it thoroughly.

2 Melt ¼ cup of the butter in a skillet. Add the bay leaf, thyme and chopped onion and sauté gently for 5 minutes, or until the onion is transparent. Add the mushrooms and seasoning. Cover and cook over low heat for 20 minutes. Add the parsley and cook for 1 more minute before removing from the heat.

3 Preheat the oven to 400°F. Using a sharp knife, split the loin lengthwise and stuff it with the mushrooms. Reserve any that are left over. Tie the loin with string and place it in a roasting tray. Dot with

the remaining butter and sprinkle it with the wine from the marinade. Bake the meat in the oven for 50-60 minutes, basting frequently while it cooks.

4 Transfer the meat to a serving dish and surround it with any leftover mushrooms. Serve with Potatoes in Green Sauce and a crisp mixed salad.

Serves 6

Potatoes in Green Sauce

¼ **cup olive oil**
2 cloves garlic, crushed
8 potatoes, peeled and thinly sliced
½ **teaspoon dried mint leaves, crumbled**
½ **cup shelled peas**
1 teaspoon salt
freshly ground black pepper
2 tablespoons finely chopped parsley

Beef Loin Stuffed with Mushrooms may seem expensive, but the tasty flavor makes it well worth trying

1 Heat the oil in a large skillet. Add the garlic and sauté until lightly browned. Add the potato slices in even layers and sprinkle them with mint. Cook gently for 1 minute. Add 3 tablespoons of water and shake the pan to distribute it evenly.

2 Continue cooking, shaking the pan occasionally and, every few minutes, adding a little more water, until the potatoes are just covered with liquid.

3 Add the peas and sprinkle with the salt and pepper. Cover and cook over low heat for about 25 minutes or until the potatoes are tender. Shake the pan now and again to prevent the potatoes from sticking. When cooked, sprinkle with the chopped parsley and serve immediately.

Serves 6

Seville Orange Cream

2 cups milk
⅔ **cup sugar**
2 egg yolks
grated rind 1 orange
6 egg whites

1 Place the milk, sugar, egg yolks and grated orange rind in a saucepan. Gently heat the mixture, stirring continually, until it is smooth and begins to thicken. Remove the saucepan from the heat.

2 Beat the egg whites until they form peaks and fold them into the orange cream. Return to the heat and cook gently, stirring continually until the mixture begins to bubble. Remove the cream from the heat and cool completely.

3 Pour the cream into 6 individual glasses and chill in the refrigerator. Serve with a bowl of whipped cream.

Serves 6

1081

Summer Spread

Sole Fingers
★
Pork Royale
★
Cranberry Tartlets
★
Pineapple Chantilly

Sole Fingers

2 lbs. sole or flounder fillets
¾ cup flour seasoned with salt
3 eggs
2¼ cups dried breadcrumbs
oil for deep frying

1 Cut the fillets into small strips 2 inches long and ¼ inch thick. Roll them in the seasoned flour and shake off the excess. Dip them in the egg and roll them in the breadcrumbs.

2 Heat the oil to 375°F. Fry the fillets for 1-2 minutes until golden. Drain and serve them with lemon wedges and a bowl of tartar sauce.

Serves 4

Pork Royale

1 6-8 lb. loin roast of pork
⅞ cup oil
¾ cup flour

Sole Fingers — nobody can resist these crispy, deep-fried fish fingers — serve them with tartar sauce

½ cup wine vinegar
salt and pepper
12 dessert apples, peeled and cored
juice 1 lemon
1¼ cups butter
dough for 9-inch pie crust
3 medium-size potatoes
2 lbs. chestnut purée
1 cup heavy cream
2¼ cups boiling milk
1 tablespoon freshly ground black pepper
6 slices sandwich bread
2 tablespoons mixed butter and oil
½ lb. cooked cranberries
¾ cup red currant jelly

For the Marinade:
2 carrots, sliced
2 onions, sliced
5 shallots, chopped
4 cloves garlic, crushed
few sprigs parsley
few juniper berries
2 teaspoons peppercorns
bay leaves
thyme
4¼ cups red wine
⅞ cup brandy
½ cup peanut oil

1 With a sharp knife, cut the pork loin from the bones and remove. Chop the bones and place them with the trimmings and loin in a deep dish. Add all the ingredients for the marinade and leave overnight.

2 The following day, remove the trimmings, bones and loin. Strain the marinade, reserving both the liquid and the vegetables.

3 Heat ½ cup of the oil in a large skillet and fry the trimmings and bones for 5 minutes. Transfer them to a dish. In the same pan, sauté the vegetables from the marinade until golden brown. Sprinkle them with ½ cup of the flour and, stirring continuously, cook for 2 minutes over low heat. Add the wine vinegar and marinade liquid and, still stirring, gradually bring the mixture to a boil. Remove the scum from the surface and return the trimmings and bones to the pan. Season, cover and simmer for 2 hours.

4 Cut the loin into 8 slices and sea-

Look 'n Cook Pork (or Venison) Royale

1 Bone the roast and reserve the trimmings **2** Marinate the meat, trimmings and bones **3** Separate the meat, bones and trimmings. Reserve the marinade **4** Fry the trimmings and bones **5** In the same pan, sauté the marinade vegetables **6, 7** and **8** Stir in the flour, vinegar and marinade liquid. Return the bones and trimmings to the pan and simmer for 2½ hours **9** Slice the loin **10** Peel and bake the apples **11** Prepare the tartlets **12** Heat the chestnut purée, butter, cream and milk **13** Strain the sauce **14** Add the pep-

per, cook for 10 minutes and strain again **15** Purée the potatoes **16** Sauté the fillet in the butter and oil. Transfer to a dish **17** Add some of the sauce to the pan and boil for a few moments. Pour the contents of the pan into the sauce **18** Arrange the slices on the croûtons. Surround them with the baked apples filled with red currant jelly and the cranberry tartlets. Pour the pepper sauce over the meat **19** Serve with the puréed potato and chestnut purée son. Preheat the oven to 400°F. Place the apples in a well-buttered dish. Sprinkle them with lemon juice and dot each one with a pat of butter. Bake for 30 minutes or until tender.

5 Roll out the pie crust on a floured board to a thickness of $\frac{1}{8}$ inch and use it to line 12 greased tartlet pans. Prick the pastry shells and bake them at the same temperature for 15 minutes. Cool on a rack.

6 Peel the potatoes and boil them in salted water for 20 minutes.

7 Meanwhile, place the chestnut purée in a saucepan. Add 1 tablespoon of butter, 2 tablespoons of heavy cream and $\frac{3}{4}$ cup of boiling milk. Heat gently, stirring continually until well blended. Remove from the heat and transfer to a warm serving dish. Keep warm.

8 When the stock is ready, pour it through a strainer into a saucepan. Discard the vegetables, bones and trimmings. Add the freshly ground pepper and simmer gently for 10 minutes. Strain the sauce again and blend in 2 teaspoons of butter. Keep it warm.

9 Strain the potatoes and mash or purée them with 4 tablespoons of butter. Gradually blend in the remaining cream and dilute if necessary with a little of the remaining milk. Transfer to a serving dish and keep warm.

10 Cut the bread slices into 8 heart-shaped croûtons. Heat the butter and oil mixture in a clean pan and fry the croûtons until golden brown. Drain them on absorbent paper and arrange on a serving dish.

11 Heat the remaining butter and oil in a clean skillet and fry the slices of meat to your taste.

12 Remove and keep warm. Pour 1 cup of the peppered sauce into the pan and stir for a few moments over high heat. Pour the contents of the pan into the rest of the sauce.

13 Fill the tart molds with the cranberries and heat them in the oven. Put a teaspoonful of red currant jelly in the center of each apple.

14 Place a slice of meat on each croûton. Surround them with the apples and the cranberry tartlets. Pour a little of the peppered sauce over the meat and serve the rest in a sauce boat. Serve with the chestnut purée and mashed potato.

Serves 8

Tip: If fresh cranberries are unavailable, fill the tartlets with cranberry sauce. To save time on the day of preparation, you can prepare the chestnut purée the day before. Cover and reheat in the oven just before serving.

Pineapple Chantilly makes a spectacular dessert which will round off a perfect dinner party with real style

Pineapple Chantilly

2 fresh pineapples
$\frac{1}{2}$ cup confectioners' sugar
2 tablespoons cherry-flavored liqueur
$2\frac{1}{4}$ cups heavy cream

1 Cut the tops off the pineapples and remove the flesh whole. Reserve the shells. Core the pineapples and cut 8 rings, $\frac{1}{2}$ inch thick, for decoration. Chop the rest and place in a bowl. Sprinkle with confectioners' sugar and marinate for 2 hours.

2 Stir the liqueur into the cream. Reserve $\frac{1}{4}$ cup of cream and carefully blend the rest with the pineapple. Pile the mixture back into the shells and chill. Arrange the pineapples on a serving plate, surrounded by the pineapple rings. Dot each ring with a little of the reserved cream and serve.

Serves 8

Candlelit Dinner

Chilled Carrot and Orange Soup

★

Cornish Hens Urubamba

★

Coconut Rice

★

Mexican Mixed Salad

★

Chocolate Banana Cups

Chilled Carrot and Orange Soup

1 lb. young carrots
⅔ cup frozen orange concentrate
1¼ cups chicken stock
salt and black pepper
¼ cup heavy cream
1 tablespoon chopped chives

1 Peel the carrots, cut them into small pieces and cook in boiling salted water for about 15 minutes, or until tender. Drain well, then whirl in a blender to form a smooth purée.

2 Add the frozen orange concentrate to the puréed carrots and mix well together. Stir in enough chicken stock to give a creamy consistency. Season to taste, then chill well.

3 Just before serving, pour the soup into 4 individual serving bowls. Stir the cream lightly until it is smooth. Using a spoon, swirl a little cream on top of each serving and sprinkle each with a few chopped chives.

Serves 4

Tip: Carrot and Orange Soup may also be served hot. Transfer the prepared soup to a clean saucepan, and heat it through gently. Do not allow it to boil as this will eliminate the flavor of the orange juice.

Cornish Hens Urubamba

1 medium or 2 small Cornish hens
¼ cup butter
1 clove garlic, crushed
½ sweet red pepper, seeded and thinly sliced
½ green pepper, seeded and thinly sliced
1½ cups mushrooms, trimmed
¼ cup corn, drained
⅓ cup apple brandy

For the Cider Sauce:
1 tablespoon butter
2 tablespoons flour
½ chicken bouillon cube dissolved in 3 tablespoons hot water
⅔ cup cider
⅔ cup light cream
salt and pepper
pinch nutmeg

1 Preheat the oven to 400°F.

2 Cut the hens into 4 serving pieces and place them in a roasting pan. Smear them with the butter and bake in the preheated oven for 25-30 minutes, basting occasionally, until golden brown.

3 Meanwhile, make the sauce: melt the butter in a pan, and stir in the flour and cook over a low heat for 2-3 minutes. Remove from the heat and gradually stir in the bouillon and cider. Bring to a boil stirring constantly, then boil the sauce rapidly for 5 minutes. Stir in the cream and simmer for a further 2 minutes. Season with salt, pepper and nutmeg and keep aside until needed.

4 Pour the fat from the cooked hens into a skillet, add the garlic, sliced peppers, mushrooms and corn, and sauté gently for 4 or 5 minutes, until the peppers are soft. Then remove from the heat. Keep the hens warm in a warm oven while serving the first course.

5 Just before serving, reheat the cider sauce. Place the Cornish hens on top of the vegetables in the pan and heat through gently. Heat the brandy in a small pan. Pour the cider sauce over the hens, pour the heated brandy around the vegetables and ignite with a long match.

6 Serve immediately with Coconut Rice and a Mexican Mixed Salad.

Serves 4

Tip: Chicken pieces also may be used in place of the Cornish hens if preferred.

Coconut Rice

2 tablespoons butter
¾ cup long grain rice
1¾ cups chicken stock
2 tablespoons raisins
½ teaspoon salt
⅔ cup shredded coconut

1 Melt the butter in a pan, add the rice and sauté gently for 2 or 3 minutes.

2 Stir in the hot stock, raisins and salt and bring to a boil. Reduce the heat, cover the pan and simmer gently for about 20 minutes, until the rice is cooked.

3 Fluff up the rice with a fork, stir in the coconut and transfer to a heated serving dish.

Serves 4

Tip: This dish can be made in advance and reheated just before serving.

Cornish Hen Urubamba, with a deliciously rich and creamy cider sauce, is flamed in brandy before it is served

Mexican Mixed Salad

1 ripe avocado
4 tomatoes
½ cucumber
1 banana
2 branches celery
4 sprigs mint
3 tablespoons oil
3 tablespoons vinegar
pinch chili powder
pinch salt

1 Peel the avocado and remove the seed, peel and seed the tomatoes, and peel the cucumber and banana. Dice all the vegetables and banana and mix them together lightly.

2 Finely chop the mint and combine it with the oil, vinegar, chili and salt. Pour it over the diced vegetables and toss lightly.

3 Just before serving, give the salad a gentle toss and divide it among 4 individual serving dishes. Serve to accompany the Cornish Hens Urubamba.

Serves 4

Tip: Red wine vinegar will give the best flavor to this salad, as well as a pinkish tinge.

Chocolate Banana Cups

3 ripe bananas
2 tablespoons rum
2¼ cups heavy cream
5½ ozs. semi-sweet chocolate, finely grated
4 scoops vanilla ice cream
½ oz. semi-sweet chocolate, finely grated (or jimmies)

1 Slice the bananas thinly and sprinkle with the rum.

2 Whip the cream until thick. Remove one-quarter of the cream, mix it with the chocolate and reserve for decoration. Add the bananas and rum to the remaining cream, and spoon the mixture into 4 individual

serving dishes.

3 Just before serving, top each dish with a scoop of ice cream. Pipe the chocolate cream around the ice cream and sprinkle with grated chocolate or jimmies.

Serves 4

Tip: Coffee ice cream would make a delicious alternative to the vanilla ice cream.

Chocolate Banana Cups. The banana is soaked in rum, mixed with cream and topped with ice cream and chocolate

Hot'n Spicy Nuts

Pass around a bowl of Hot 'n Spicy Nuts with your pre-dinner drinks. Melt 2 tablespoons butter in a small pan. Add ¾ cup mixed nuts and sauté for 3 or 4 minutes. Remove from the heat, stir in a few shakes of celery salt and a generous pinch of chili powder and serve immediately. They're sure to give your guests a suggestion of the sumptuous meal to follow.

Entertaining: Buffets

Bass Melbourne

Cocktail Buffets

An ideal cocktail party — or any gathering where alcoholic drinks are being served — should include some food. Although guests will probably not want to eat much, a little food modifies the effect of the alcohol and increases its appreciation. Small, savory, tempting dishes are ideal. Served in bite-sized portions that can be held in the hand and eaten without mess, they will help to make any party a success. Serve them with pretty canapés such as olives, nuts, and salami slices.

Tarama Tartlets

½ lb. puff pastry, fresh or frozen
  and thawed
¼ lb. smoked cod roe
2 slices white bread
1 tablespoon milk
⅓ cup olive oil
2 tablespoons lemon juice
1 tablespoon grated onion
1 clove garlic, finely chopped
  (optional)
salt and pepper

1 Preheat the oven to 425°F. On a lightly floured board, roll out the pastry to ¼ inch thick. Using a 2-inch fluted round pastry cutter, cut out small circles and place them in a greased tartlet tin. Bake for about 15 minutes until risen and golden brown. Remove from the oven and allow to cool.

2 Mash the roe with a fork in a mixing bowl.

3 Remove the crusts from the slices of bread. Soak the slices in milk and crumble them. Mix the bread with the cod roe.

4 Gradually beat in the olive oil and the lemon juice, beating constantly to make a smooth mixture.

Add the grated onion and the garlic, if wished. Season with a little salt and pepper. Continue beating, adding a little water to make the mixture more fluffy, and adjusting the lemon juice and seasoning to taste.

5 When the mixture is smooth and creamy, place it in a decorator's bag and pipe it in swirls into the tartlets. Chill if not served immediately.

Makes 10-12

Tip: If you have a blender, the mixing can be done much more easily and the result will be smoother. Add more oil or water in small quantities, if necessary.

Cheese Puffs

14 ozs. puff pastry, fresh or frozen
  and thawed
½ lb. Gruyère cheese, sliced
2 egg yolks
1 tablespoon milk
freshly ground black pepper

1 Preheat the oven to 425°F. On a floured board, roll out the pastry to ¼ inch thick. Cut it into squares of about 1½ inches. Cut the cheese into squares of the same size.

2 Beat the egg yolks lightly with the milk. Brush the tops of the pastry squares with egg wash. Place a square of cheese on a square of pastry, dust with freshly ground black pepper, and top with another square of pastry, egg side uppermost. Repeat until all the pastry and cheese are used.

3 Place the cheese squares on a greased baking sheet, and bake for about 15 minutes until golden brown. Serve warm or cold.

Makes 10–12

Salmon Croissants

½ lb. puff pastry, fresh or frozen
  and thawed
¼ lb. canned salmon
2 tablespoons butter
¼ cup flour
1¼ cups milk
salt and pepper
1 egg yolk, beaten

1 Preheat the oven to 425°F. On a floured board, roll out the puff pastry to ¼ inch thick and cut it into triangles with sides about 4 inches long.

2 Drain the juice from the canned salmon and reserve it. Remove any skin or bones from the salmon and crush it with a fork.

3 Make a thick white sauce by melting the butter in a saucepan and stirring in the flour. Cook for a minute, then gradually stir in the salmon liquor and enough milk to form a very thick, smooth sauce. Season to taste with salt and pepper. Beat in the salmon meat.

4 Spoon a little of the mixture into the middle of each pastry triangle. Roll up the triangles, starting from a straight side and rolling toward the opposite point, completely enclosing the salmon filling.

5 Twist each piece into a crescent shape and brush the top with beaten egg. Place the croissants on a greased baking sheet and bake for 15-20 minutes until golden brown on top. Serve hot or cold.

Makes 10–12

Tip: For an alternative fish filling: with a fork, mash the drained fish from 1 or 2 large cans of sardines with 1-2 tablespoons catsup. Season with cayenne pepper. Add a few crushed anchovy fillets if wished.

Ideas for party snacks include Cheese Puffs (bottom right), Salmon Croissants, Tarama Tartlets and Sausage Rolls (center), and Toast with Liver Pâté

Salmon Boats

two 9-inch pie crusts
¼ lb. smoked salmon, thinly sliced
1 lemon
¼ lb. salmon
¼ cup heavy cream
salt and pepper
pinch paprika

1 Preheat the oven to 375°F. Roll out the dough thinly. With a fluted boat-shaped pastry cutter, cut out the boats, and place the pastry pieces in greased oval tins. Prick the bottoms of the pastry shells with a fork. Bake for 10-15 minutes until crisp and lightly browned. Cool.

2 Meanwhile, cut the smoked salmon slices into boat shapes, slightly larger than the pastry molds. Reserve any trimmings. Sprinkle the salmon pieces with the juice of half the lemon.

3 Drain the canned salmon and discard any skin or bones. Flake the flesh with a fork. Finely dice the reserved smoked salmon trimmings and mix them with the salmon.

4 Mix the salmon with the heavy cream and season with salt and pepper and a little paprika. Spoon the mixture into the pastry boats. Cover each one with a piece of smoked salmon, and decorate with 'butterflies' of lemon cut from the remaining lemon half. Serve at once.

Makes 8–12

Asparagus Boats

two 9-inch pie crusts
3 eggs
⅓ cup mayonnaise
1 teaspoon prepared mustard
36 asparagus tips

Salmon Boats are an attractive, extravagant snack to pass around to your guests at an elegant cocktail party

1 Prepare the pastry boats as described in Salmon Boats.

2 Hard-boil the eggs for 10 minutes. Remove the shells and finely chop the eggs.

3 Mix the chopped egg with the mayonnaise and mustard. Spoon the mixture into the prepared pastry boats.

4 Drain the asparagus tips and arrange them in an attractive pattern on top of the filled pastry boats. Serve cold.

Makes 8–12

Bacon and Banana Kebabs

3 bananas
juice ½ lemon
2 tablespoons catsup
1 tablespoon vinegar
1 tablespoon dark brown sugar
¼ lb. thinly sliced lean bacon

1 Peel the bananas and cut them into 1½-inch lengths. Sprinkle them with lemon juice.

2 Mix the catsup and vinegar over low heat in a saucepan and add the sugar. Heat gently, stirring, until melted and blended.

3 Coat the banana pieces with the sauce. Wrap a piece of bacon around each piece of banana to completely enclose it, and fix in place with a toothpick, passed through the banana.

4 Place the kebabs under the broiler and cook, turning them occasionally, until the bacon is lightly browned and crisp. Serve hot.

Serves 6

Tip: Similar small kebabs may be made using a variety of fillings. For a cheese 'n bacon kebab, cut pieces of Gruyère cheese about 1 inch square and spread with French

4 Mix the cooked mushrooms with the cheese sauce. Spoon the mixture into the prepared pastry boats and sprinkle the tops with the rest of the grated cheese. Place the boats under the broiler for a few minutes until the cheese is melted and golden. Serve at once.

Makes 8–12

Cocktail Kebabs

1 pineapple
$\frac{1}{4}$ lb. thinly sliced lean bacon
$\frac{1}{4}$ lb. cocktail sausages
2 tablespoons butter

For the Sauce:
2 tablespoons catsup
2 tablespoons fruit chutney
2 teaspoons Worcestershire
  sauce
1 teaspoon vinegar or lemon juice
few drops chili sauce

1 Peel the pineapple and remove the core. Cut the flesh into 1-inch cubes.

2 Cut the bacon slices into pieces, long enough to be wrapped around a pineapple cube and fixed in place with a toothpick.

3 Cut the cocktail sausages into 1-inch lengths. Spear a piece of sausage together with a piece of pineapple on each toothpick.

4 Melt the butter in a skillet and lightly fry the kebabs; or, brush them with melted butter and broil them until the bacon and sausage pieces are cooked.

5 Meanwhile, make the sauce. Beat together all the ingredients or mix them in a blender. Pour the sauce in a sauce boat or small dish and serve with the hot kebabs.

Serves about 12

mustard. Wrap in bacon and broil. Alternatively, wrap the bacon around large pineapple chunks.

Cocktail Kebabs—serve them with celery chunks and succulent dates filled with cream cheese, gherkins and paprika

1 cup grated cheese

1 Prepare the pastry boats as described in Salmon Boats.

2 Clean the mushrooms and cut them into thin slices. Place them in a saucepan with half of the butter and cook over low heat for about 3 minutes, until softened and lightly browned.

3 In another pan, melt the rest of the butter and cook the flour for 1 minute. Gradually add the milk, stirring constantly, to make a smooth thick sauce. Season with salt and pepper. Stir in half of the cheese.

Cheese and Mushroom Boats

two 9-inch pie crusts
$\frac{1}{2}$ lb. mushrooms
2 tablespoons butter
1 tablespoon flour
$\frac{3}{4}$ cup milk
salt and pepper

1093

Party Pâtés & Dips

Dips and pâtés are ever–popular party fare, either as hors d'oeuvres before a quiet dinner party or as a snack to be enjoyed throughout the evening. Easy to prepare, they can be made days before the event and, if covered, will keep indefinitely in the refrigerator. Your guests can help themselves to a slice of French bread and pâté or scoop into a colorful dip with crackers, crudités or even the humble potato chip. Try serving your favorite cold dip in a hollowed-out red cabbage, grapefruit, eggplant, or even a lovely firm pineapple.

Chive Dip

4 ozs. cream cheese
2 tablespoons chopped chives
1 tablespoon light cream, if
  necessary

1 Blend the cream cheese and chives to a soft cream, adding the cream if necessary.

2 Serve in a bowl, surrounded with French bread, chips or crackers.

Makes $\frac{2}{3}$ cup

Variations

The cream cheese dip can be endlessly varied. Try mashing 2 small avocados with the cheese or blending some chopped red and green peppers with a little seasoning. Mix in $\frac{1}{4}$ cup of Roquefort or blue cheese with the juice of half a lemon. Try adding 2 tablespoons of tomato purée with a dash of chili sauce and perhaps some corn.

Spanish Country Pâté

$\frac{1}{2}$ lb. chicken livers, minced
1 lb. pork liver, minced
$\frac{1}{2}$ lb. beef, minced
1$\frac{1}{4}$ lbs. pork, minced
$\frac{3}{4}$ lb. bacon, minced
1 tablespoon salt
pepper
1 teaspoon ground mace
1 tablespoon chopped fresh sage
  and dill or 2 teaspoons dried
  herbs
2 tablespoons sherry
$\frac{1}{4}$ cup brandy
3 cloves garlic, crushed
$\frac{1}{3}$ cup stuffed green olives

1 Preheat the oven to 300°F. Mix all the ingredients, except the olives, until well blended. Divide the pâté between two well-greased 3$\frac{1}{4}$ cup dishes or loaf pans.

2 Disperse the olives throughout the pâté, at different levels.

3 Cover the dishes with aluminum foil and place them in a roasting pan with 2 inches of water and bake for 2 hours. Cool.

4 Refrigerate the pâtés for 1-2 hours before turning them out onto a serving dish.

Serves 8–10

Liver and Olive Pâté

6 slices lean bacon
$\frac{1}{4}$ lb. chicken livers
$\frac{1}{2}$ lb. pork liver
$\frac{3}{4}$ lb. minced pork
$\frac{1}{2}$ lb. pork fat
$\frac{1}{4}$ lb. minced beef
2 cloves garlic, crushed
2 teaspoons mixed dried sage and
  dill
1$\frac{1}{2}$ teaspoons salt
1 teaspoon pepper
1 egg, beaten

6 stuffed green olives

1 Stretch the bacon slices with a round-bladed knife. Use the slices to line a 1-lb. loaf pan.

2 Mince the chicken livers, pork liver, pork and fat. Add the beef, garlic, herbs, salt, pepper, egg and olives and beat well.

3 Preheat the oven to 300°F. Press the mixture into the prepared pan. Stand it in a roasting pan with 1 inch of water and bake for 2 hours. Remove the pâté from the roasting pan and cool thoroughly.

4 Turn out onto a plate and serve with sliced tomato and crisp lettuce.

Serves 8–10

Mackerel Pâté

4 smoked mackerel fillets
juice 1 lemon
4 ozs. cream cheese
$\frac{1}{2}$ lb. butter, melted
salt and pepper
4 stuffed green olives
1 slice lemon

1 Skin and flake the mackerel fillets. Put the fish, lemon juice, cream cheese and melted butter in a blender and blend to a purée. (Alternatively, mash the fillets with a fork and pass them through a sieve before blending them with the lemon juice, cream cheese and butter.) Season to taste.

2 Pour the purée into a 1-lb. loaf pan or suitable serving dish. Smooth the top with a knife and decorate with the sliced olives. Chill and serve garnished with a slice of lemon.

Serves 8

Spanish Country Pâté (top left), Mackerel Pâté (top right) and Liver and Olive Pâté all go down well at a buffet party

Look 'n Cook Eggplant Dip

1 The ingredients: eggplant, parsley, garlic, onion, cream cheese, lemon and seasoning **2** Prick the eggplant with a fork before baking it in the oven **3** Halve it lengthwise and scoop out the flesh **4** Blend the pulp with the cream cheese, chopped onion and parsley and the juice of half a lemon **5** Season to taste **6** Spoon the dip into a bowl and serve with crisp crudités

Eastern Dip

¼ lb. shallots, minced
½ teaspoon fresh coriander
¼ cup chopped parsley
2 tablespoons chopped fresh
  ginger
1 teaspoon soy sauce
2 tablespoons chopped canned
  water chestnuts
1 cup sour cream
2 tablespoons mayonnaise

1 In a bowl, thoroughly blend all the ingredients.

2 Pile the mixture into a serving bowl and serve with sliced raw mushrooms and raw cauliflower.

Makes approximately 1½ cups

Hot Cheese Dip

¾ lb. Cheddar cheese
¼ lb. Roquefort cheese
2 tablespoons butter
½ teaspoon Worcestershire sauce
½ teaspoon prepared mustard
pinch salt
½ clove garlic, crushed
1 cup flat beer

1 Combine all the dip ingredients in a bowl and melt them over a pan of hot water.

2 Pour the dip immediately into a serving bowl and serve with bite-size pieces of celery, cubes of fresh bread or croûtons.

Makes approximately 2 cups

Tip: Always have a number of long forks available for your friends to dip the bread or crudités into the cheese. This will save burned fingers and a messy table.

Eggplant Dip

1 large eggplant
1 onion, chopped
1 clove garlic, crushed
1 tablespoon chopped parsley
juice ½ lemon
8 ozs. cream cheese
salt and pepper

1 Preheat the oven to 375°F. Prick the eggplant all over with a fork and bake it in the oven for 45 minutes or until very soft. Cool it under cold water and halve it lengthwise. Use a tablespoon to scoop out the pulp.

2 In a bowl, blend the eggplant with the onion, garlic, chopped parsley, lemon juice and cream cheese. Season to taste.

3 Pile the dip into a serving dish on a plate. Garnish with a sprig of parsley and serve surrounded by sliced carrots, cauliflower florets, celery, cucumber and mushrooms.

Serves 4

Tip: Instead of baking the eggplant, you can broil it for 20 minutes, or until the outside is black and the flesh has collapsed.

Eggplant Dip — your guests can use the crisp crudités to help themselves to this chunky-textured dip

Party Buffets

The following beautifully presented buffet dishes have been designed as composite meals but they can be interchanged and, of course, how many dishes you prepare will depend on the number of people you invite. Serve the buffets with bowls of colorful fresh fruit and your favorite punch.

Celery, Walnut and Orange Salad

rind 1 orange
1 tablespoon butter
2 tablespoons all-purpose flour
juice 1 orange
salt and pepper
1 tablespoon sugar
2 teaspoons vinegar
1 bunch celery
½ cup walnuts, chopped

1 Place the orange rind with 1¼ cups of water in a saucepan. Simmer for 10 minutes. Strain and reserve the liquid.

2 Melt the butter in a saucepan and stir in the flour. Gradually stir in the orange juice and reserved orange water. Bring to a boil, stirring continuously. Season and stir in the sugar and vinegar. Cool.

3 Slice the celery, mix it with the walnuts in a bowl and pour on the orange dressing. Toss and chill.

Serves 10–12

Tip: For a fruitier flavor, try including 6 canned apricot halves, drained and finely sliced. Add the apricots to the celery and walnuts before pouring on the orange dressing.

Green Bean Salad

2 tablespoons butter
¼ cup flour
1¼ cups milk
salt and pepper
1 tablespoon vinegar
1 lb. fresh green beans
12 ozs. cooked asparagus, drained
4 large tomatoes, sliced
½ large cucumber, peeled and diced
1 tablespoon chopped parsley

1 Melt the butter in a saucepan. Stir in the flour and cook for 1-2 minutes. Gradually stir in the milk and bring to a boil. Season, stir in the vinegar, cover and leave to cool.

2 Cut the beans into 2-inch lengths and cook them for 5 minutes in boiling salted water. Cut the asparagus into 1-inch lengths. Drain the beans and leave them to cool.

3 Arrange the tomatoes around the rim of a serving bowl and place the beans, asparagus, cucumber and parsley in the center. Pour on the sauce and toss lightly.

Serves 10–12

Orange Meringue Cake

¾ lb. butter
3 cups sugar
10 large eggs
3¼ cups self-rising flour
¾ cup all-purpose flour
grated rind 2 oranges
2¼ cups milk
juice 1 orange
3 tablespoons orange liqueur
1⅓ cups pineapple jam
4 slices orange

1 Preheat the oven to 375°F. Place the butter, 1½ cups of the sugar, 6 eggs and the self-rising flour in a mixing bowl. Beat well until smooth and spoon the mixture into a greased and lined 11-inch cake pan. Bake in the center of the oven for 1 hour, or until well-risen and firm to the touch. Cool on a rack.

2 Put ⅓ cup sugar, the all-purpose flour, 4 egg yolks and the finely grated orange rind in a mixing bowl. Beat well, adding a little of the milk.

3 Bring the rest of the milk to a boil and, stirring continuously, gradually pour it onto the orange mixture. Return to the saucepan and bring the sauce to a boil, still stirring. Cool slightly, stir in the orange juice, cover and chill.

4 Cut the cake into 3 layers and pour the liqueur over each one. Place the bottom layer on a large baking sheet. Spread with half of the jam and half of the orange cream. Put the center layer on top and spread it with the remaining jam and cream. Top with the remaining layer.

5 Preheat the oven to 425°F. Beat 4 egg whites until very stiff and mix in the remaining sugar, one tablespoon at a time and beating well between each addition.

6 Spread a smooth layer of the meringue over the top of the cake. Place the rest in a decorator's bag fitted with a large star nozzle and pipe lines of meringue around the side. Bake in the oven for 2-3 minutes until the meringue is lightly golden. Cool, decorate with the orange slices and serve.

Serves 10–12

Front, left to right: Green Bean Salad; Celery, Walnut and Orange Salad; and Curried Pasta Salad. Behind: Chicken Vol-au-Vent; Orange Meringue Gâteau; and Cauliflower Salad

Chicken Vol-au-Vent

one 5-lb. chicken
2 bay leaves
salt and pepper
1 small onion, skinned
1 carrot, peeled
2 lbs. 2 ozs. puff pastry, fresh
  or frozen and thawed
1 egg, beaten
¼ cup butter
½ cup flour
1¼ cups milk
1 chicken bouillon cube
½ lb. mushrooms, washed and
  sliced
⅔ cup light cream

1 Wash the chicken and giblets and place them in a large saucepan. Add the bay leaves, salt, pepper, onion and carrot. Just cover the chicken with water and cook gently for 1½–2 hours.

2 Preheat the oven to 450°F. Roll out the pastry to a thickness of ¾ inch and cut out an 11-inch round, using a springform-pan ring or saucepan lid as a guide.

3 Cutting almost through the pastry, cut a smaller round in the center about 9 inches in diameter. Brush the pastry with beaten egg and bake it in the center of the oven for 40–45 minutes until well-risen and crisp. Cool.

4 Cut out the 'lid' and scoop out any uncooked pastry.

5 Drain the stock from the chicken, reserving 1¼ cups. Remove the chicken meat from the bones and cut into chunks.

6 Melt the butter in a saucepan. Stir in the flour and cook for 1-2 minutes. Gradually stir in the chicken stock and milk. Add the bouillon cube and, stirring continuously, bring to a boil. Add the mushrooms and simmer for 10 minutes before stirring in the chicken and cream.

7 Fill the vol-au-vent with the chicken mixture and replace the lid. Serve hot or cold.

Serves 10–12

Cauliflower Salad

2 tablespoons butter
¼ cup flour
1¼ cups milk
salt and pepper
1 bunch watercress, chopped
1 tablespoon chopped chives
1 tablespoon mayonnaise
1 large cauliflower
10 radishes, sliced

1 Melt the butter in a saucepan. Stir in the flour and cook gently for 1-2 minutes. Gradually stir in the milk and bring to a boil. Season, cover and cool. Stir the watercress, chives and mayonnaise into the sauce.

2 Divide the cauliflower into florets and cook them in salted water for 5 minutes. Drain and cool. Place the cauliflower and radishes on a bed of lettuce leaves in a salad bowl. Pour on the sauce and toss lightly. Chill and serve.

Serves 10–12

Curried Pasta Salad

1 onion, chopped
1 tablespoon corn oil
¼ cup flour
1¼ cups beef stock
1 tablespoon curry powder
1 tablespoon catsup
2 small peeled tomatoes
salt and pepper
1 onion, sliced
½ large cucumber, diced
2 cups pasta, cooked
lemon wedges

1 Sauté the chopped onion in the oil until soft. Stir in the flour and cook for 1 minute. Gradually stir in the stock and add the curry powder, catsup and tomatoes. Season and simmer for 20 minutes. Cool.

2 Place the sliced onion, cucumber and pasta in a large bowl. Pour on the cooled curry sauce and toss gently. Serve with lemon wedges.

Serves 10–12

Salmon and Avocado Flan

1⅔ cups flour
salt and pepper
6 tablespoons butter
4 large eggs
1 tablespoon corn oil
1 small onion, chopped
2 scallions, minced
¾ lb. canned red salmon
milk
⅓ cup grated Cheddar
1 ripe avocado
1 lemon, sliced

1 Preheat the oven to 425°F. Sift the flour and a pinch of salt into a bowl and rub in the butter. Mix to a stiff dough with one of the eggs and a little water. Roll out the dough and use it to line an 8-inch flan pan. Trim the edges.

2 Heat the oil in a pan and sauté the onion and scallion until soft. Drain.

3 Drain the salmon, reserving the liquid. Flake the salmon and add the milk to make 1¾ cups liquid.

4 Beat the remaining eggs and salmon liquid. Add the fish, onions and cheese. Season and spoon into the pan.

5 Cook the flan in the center of the oven for 45 minutes until golden brown and set. Cool.

6 Peel, halve and pit the avocado, and cut it lengthwise into slices. Decorate the flan with avocado and lemon slices and garnish with parsely.

Serves 8–10

Salmon and Avocado Flan has an economical filling of canned salmon, milk and cheese, with an avocado and orange garnish

Pork and Veal Loaf

3 tablespoons oil
¼ cup butter
1 onion, chopped
4 branches celery, chopped
2 cloves garlic, crushed
1¼ cups red wine
5 slices white bread with crusts
  removed
1¼ lbs. minced pork
1¼ lbs. minced veal
½ lb. sausage meat
salt and pepper
pinch allspice
pinch thyme
2 bay leaves, crushed
3 eggs, beaten
1 tomato, thinly sliced
few sprigs parsley

1 Preheat the oven to 325°F. Heat the oil and butter and sauté the onion, celery and garlic until soft. Add the wine and simmer for 5 minutes.

2 Crumble the bread and add to the pan with the meats, seasonings, herbs and egg. Mix well.

3 Spoon the mixture into a well-buttered loaf pan and bake for 1½–2 hours. You can baste the loaf with a little warm wine.

4 Turn out the Pork and Veal Loaf and allow to cool. Decorate the top with overlapping tomato slices and sprigs of parsley.

Serves 10–12

Curried Chicken Salad

2 tablespoons butter
¼ cup flour
1¼ cups milk
⅔ cup chicken stock
1 teaspoon curry powder
salt and pepper
pinch paprika
grated rind 1 lemon
⅔ cup light cream
⅓ cup raisins

2 cups cooked chicken meat, diced
  or cut in strips
2 tablespoons chopped parsley

1 Make a roux with the butter and flour and cook gently for 2 minutes without browning. Gradually add the milk and chicken stock, stirring all the time, until the sauce boils and becomes thick and smooth.

2 Add the curry powder, seasoning and lemon rind. Reduce the heat and simmer gently.

3 Remove from the heat and beat in the cream. Then mix in the raisins and chicken meat.

4 Arrange the chicken curry on a serving plate and surround with a border of saffron rice. Sprinkle the top with parsley and serve either hot or cold.

Serves 8–10

Celery à la Grecque

4 celery hearts
juice 2 lemons
2¼ cups water
⅔ cup olive oil
1 bay leaf
12 peppercorns
12 coriander seeds
pinch salt
1¼ cups mayonnaise
2 tablespoons tarragon vinegar
16 anchovy fillets
8 black olives

1 Cut each celery heart in half and wash thoroughly.

2 Place the lemon juice, water, oil, bay leaf and seasonings in a pan and bring to a boil. Add the celery hearts, cover, and simmer until tender. Drain and cool.

3 Arrange the celery on a dish. Mix the mayonnaise and vinegar and coat each celery heart. Decorate with the anchovy fillets and olives.

Serves 8

Grape Flan

12 ozs. cream cheese
juice 2 oranges
grated rind 1 orange
one 9-inch baked pie crust
¼ lb. green grapes, halved and
  seeded
¼ lb. purple grapes, halved and
  seeded
1 tablespoon sugar
2 tablespoons water

1 Mix together the cream cheese, orange juice and rind. Spread this mixture across the base of the pie crust.

2 Arrange 2 triangles of green grapes and 2 of purple grapes on top of the filling, facing inward.

3 Boil the sugar and water until syrupy and brush over the grapes. Serve with whipped cream.

Serves 8

Guacamole Dip

2 ripe avocados, peeled
juice 1 lemon
1 clove garlic, crushed
4 tomatoes, skinned, seeded
  and chopped
½ onion, chopped
2 branches celery, chopped
1 tablespoon chopped parsley
2 tablespoons olive oil
salt and pepper

1 Mash the avocados and blend with the other ingredients.

2 Chill and serve with crudités — celery and carrot sticks, and chunks of pepper.

Serves 8–10

A delicious buffet spread to suit everybody's taste: Grape Flan, a Mandarin Cheesecake, Pork and Veal Loaf, a crunchy salad, Guacamole Dip, Celery à la Grecque and Curried Chicken Salad

Grapefruit Cocktail

8 grapefruit
2 red apples, cored and sliced
½ cup walnuts, coarsely chopped
¼ lb. blue cheese, cubed
¼ lb. green seedless grapes
¼ cup oil
2 tablespoons lemon juice

1 Cut the top off each grapefruit by cutting round the sides in a zig-zag pattern. Scoop out the flesh and pith and remove the membrane between each section.

2 Mix with the apple, walnuts, cheese and grapes and blend in the oil and lemon juice.

3 Fill each grapefruit shell with this mixture. Chill and serve.

Serves 8

Tip: The best blue cheese to use in this recipe is Roquefort.

Mandarin Cheesecake

1¼ cups crushed butter cookies
⅔ cup butter, melted
¼ cup sugar
pinch cinnamon
1 lb. cream cheese
1⅓ cups confectioners' sugar
1¼ cups heavy cream
1 lb. canned mandarin oranges, drained
2 tablespoons unflavored gelatin
grated rind 1 lemon
1 oz. semi-sweet chocolate, grated

1 Mix together the crushed cookies, butter, sugar and cinnamon. Press firmly into a 9-inch springform pan and chill.

2 Blend the cream cheese, sugar and cream. Chop half of the man-

---

Grapefruit Cocktail, with its tasty sweet and savory stuffing of blue cheese, fruits and walnuts, tastes delicious

darins and mix into the cheese mixture.

3 Soften the gelatin in a little warm water and add with the lemon rind to the mixture.

4 Line the sides of the pan with wax paper and pour in the mixture. Level the top and chill until set.

5 Remove from the pan and decorate with the reserved mandarins and grated chocolate.

Serves 8–10

Stuffed Melon Salad

1 ripe avocado, peeled, halved and pitted
juice 1 lemon
one 3-lb. chicken, roasted
1 cantaloupe (or other variety) melon
1 green pepper, seeded and cut in strips
1 small onion, chopped
⅓ cup raisins
salt and pepper
1 cup cooked rice

1 Cut the avocado flesh into chunks, cover with lemon juice and put aside.

2 Cut the chicken meat into strips. Cut around the top of the melon in a zig-zag design and remove the lid. With a melon baller, hollow out the flesh to form balls.

3 Mix the avocado, chicken, melon balls, pepper, onion, raisins, seasoning and rice. Fill the melon shell with this mixture and serve the rest separately or use it to stuff another melon. Surround the melon(s) with a coleslaw salad and serve with mayonnaise.
Serves 8

Stuffed Melon Salad using various melons is served with crunchy coleslaw. Your guests can help themselves to the delicious rice filling

Look 'n Cook Stuffed Melon Salad

1 The ingredients: melon of your choice, roast chicken, avocado, green pepper, onion, rice and raisins 2 Halve the avocado, remove the pit Sald cut the pulp into cubes 3 Pour the lemon juice over the avocado and put aside 4 Carve the chicken and cut the meat into strips. Seed and slice the green pepper and peel and chop the onion 5 With a sharp knife, cut around the top of the melon in a zig-zag design and remove the lid

6 Using a melon baller, scoop out the melon to form small balls **7** Meanwhile, cook the rice and mix in a large bowl with the avocado, chicken strips, chopped onion, strips of pepper, raisins and melon balls. Mix well together and season with salt and pepper **8** Spoon into the hollowed-out melon

Birthday Buffet

Lotus Blossom Chicken

Bass Melbourne

Spiced Sirloin Sandringham

Muscovite Salad

Buffet Bouchées

Orange Surprises

Exotic Fruit Salad

Marzipan

This birthday buffet spread looks impressive and difficult to prepare but appearances can be deceptive and it is relatively easy when you know how. Although our buffet is for a 21st birthday celebration, you can, of course, prepare this spread for any special occasion or party. The beauty of this menu is that many of the dishes can be prepared and cooked in advance and frozen until the big day. So if you have a freezer, you can save yourself a lot of time and trouble. For example, the brioches, bread rolls and pastry shells can be made beforehand and frozen until needed, then thawed and topped with fresh fillings and spreads or frozen and thawed sauces. The cake, of course, will benefit from being stored in an airtight tin for several weeks before icing.

The most important thing to remember when you are planning a buffet is that all the food should be eaten with forks, spoons or fingers — there should be no necessity for knives. Most probably, it will be eaten standing up and each guest will need a free hand to hold the plate. Be sensible about including chicken and other meats on your buffet spread. If possible, carve them in advance, preferably with an electric carving knife, if you have one. It not only takes the difficulty out of carving, but you can also slice thinner portions so there is less waste and more portions to go around. If you are serving whole legs or wings of poultry, it is perfectly fine and acceptable etiquette to pick them up and eat them with your fingers.

Setting the table and decorating are also important points. It is a good idea to make sure that the table is approachable from all sides — this will cut down on long lines for

food. Cover it with a pretty table-cloth and provide plenty of napkins. Paper ones are best — they are cheap and easily disposed of. If you can, arrange the forks and spoons down both sides so that they are accessible. Set the table carefully with shallower dishes at the front, deeper ones at the back so that when people lean over they do not dangle their sleeves in the food. There should be plenty of serving spoons for people to help themselves. You can stand the serving plates on liner plates so that spilled and dribbled food is neatly caught and does not mark the cloth. You may use attractive china serving dishes and provide your guests with disposable paper plates. It will lessen the washing up afterward.

Cut a slice out of flans and cakes to encourage guests to go ahead and help themselves — they are sometimes inhibited about digging in or may even take too large portions so that there is not enough to go around. Cover the table loosely with a cloth or wrap the food in foil until it is time to serve — some food dries out very quickly.

Last, but not least, choose with care the dishes you make. Provide something to suit everybody's taste, whether vegetarian or weight-watcher. Individual dishes should be light, not too rich or heavy. The accent should be on attractive colors and presentation. Garnish savory dishes with sprigs of parsley and watercress and lemon wedges and slices. Cream, whipped and piped, will always improve the appearance of desserts and cakes. Also, remember that most people will not try every dish and that they eat smaller portions than at a normal dinner. Therefore, for a party of 20 guests, you need not provide 20 portions of absolutely everything. Strategically place bowls of nuts, olives, crackers and small hors d'oeuvres around the room so that your guests can nibble before the food is served.

1 *Marzipan*
2 *Birthday Cake*
3 *Muscovite Salad*
4 *Fish Mayonnaise*
5 *Bass Melbourne*
6 *Orange Surprises*
7 *Lotus Blossom Chicken*
8 *Party Rolls and Brioches*
9 *Exotic Fruit Salad*
10 *Buffet Bouchées*

Party Rolls and Brioches

Small rolls and brioches are ideal party fare. They can be filled with an enormous variety of tempting foods; they are easy to prepare and easy to eat. To fill brioches, first lift off the topknots, then remove some of the soft center to make space for a filling. The fillings shown here are only a few of the possibilities; those shown in the bouchées (bite-sized pastry shells), opposite, could also be used in soft rolls, and vice versa. The presentation of rolls and bouchées is important — arrange them on a large serving dish, and garnish with lettuce leaves, or sprigs of watercress or parsley for a fresh effect.

Creamy Eggs

Place 4 eggs in a pan and cover with cold water. Add 1 teaspoon salt and bring to a boil. Reduce the heat and simmer for 8 minutes. Cool the hard-boiled eggs under running cold water and then remove the shells. Finely chop the eggs and mix them with ⅔ cup mayonnaise, 2 teaspoons mustard, one finely chopped small onion, and seasoning to taste. Spread the mixture over halved rolls and garnish each roll with an anchovy fillet and a halved black olive, or three capers arranged in a row and a sprig of cress.

Ham Salad

Finely chop: ¼ lb. lean ham, half a dill pickle, 1 small onion, and 1 cooked potato. Mix these ingredients into ⅔ cup mayonnaise. Stir in a pinch of paprika, salt and pepper to taste, and 1 tablespoon finely chopped parsley or chives. Spoon onto rolls.

Spring Salmon

Drain ¼ lb. canned salmon. Remove any skin or pieces of bone and mash the meat with a fork. Stir in the juice of half a lemon, 1 tablespoon cream, and a dash of paprika. For extra piquancy, add a few drops of anchovy paste and some chopped scallions. Spread on rolls.

Tongue and Asparagus

Drain cooked asparagus tips. Curl

Party Rolls and Brioches can be topped and filled with a wide variety of savory, creamy mixtures and sauces

half a slice of finely sliced tongue round three or four asparagus tips, and arrange on a roll.

Cottage Cheese

Mash ⅔ cup cottage cheese with a fork. Finely chop three pickled cocktail onions and mix them into the cheese. Spread on rolls and garnish with a lettuce leaf or a slice of fresh orange.

Piquant Pâté

Cream together ¼ lb. soft liver pâté with ¼ cup heavy cream. Mix in a finely chopped dill pickle, some chopped capers and a few drops of

chili sauce. Place in a decorator's bag with a star nozzle and pipe into the hollowed brioches. Replace the topknots of the brioches.

Avocado Surprise

Remove the pulp of an avocado and cream it with the juice of half a lemon. Spoon the mixture into hollowed brioches. Beat ⅔ cup cream cheese with ¼ cup heavy cream. Place in a decorator's bag with a star nozzle and pipe swirls of cheese on top of the avocado filling. Top with the topknots of the brioches.

Shrimp and Cucumber

Butter some rolls and arrange slices of cucumber on them. In the middle, place an overlapping row of peeled, deveined, cooked shrimp. Alternatively, mix ¼ lb. shrimp with

Buffet Bouchées are bite-sized puff pastry shells filled with different colored roe and savory mixtures

$\frac{2}{3}$ cup mayonnaise and 2 teaspoons catsup and place this mixture on the cucumber slices.

Sardine and Watercress
Drain the oil from a large can of sardines. Arrange one or two sardines on each roll and top with a sprig of washed watercress and a half slice of lemon. If wished, the sardines can be mashed with 2 tablespoons mayonnaise and 2 teaspoons tomato paste.

Mustard Spread
Mix together 1 tablespoon prepared French mustard with 2 tablespoons mayonnaise. Add 1 tablespoon each of: finely chopped sweet red pepper, green pepper, onion, dill pickle, and corn. Spread on rolls; top, if wished, with a slice of tongue or thinly sliced cheese, garnished with tomato.

Buffet Bouchées

Bouchées — small pastry shells — are easy to make, but when catering for a large party you may prefer to buy ready-made frozen ones. Fill them with some of these delicious ideas.

As with party rolls and brioches, presentation of these bouchées is important — they should look as delicious as they taste. Pretty paper napkins will serve as well as plates for this finger-food — and save on washing-up too!

Duxelles
Finely chop: 2 cups mushrooms, 2 ozs. lean ham, and half an onion. Sauté the onion for 1 minute in 3 tablespoons butter, then stir in the mushrooms and ham and cook for 3 more minutes, stirring, over low heat. Add 1 tablespoon finely chopped parsley, 1 teaspoon tomato paste, and seasoning to taste. Allow to cool and spoon into the pastry shells.

Salmon Cream
Drain $\frac{1}{2}$ lb. canned salmon, remove any skin or bone, and flake the meat. Mix it with $\frac{1}{4}$ cup heavy cream and 2 tablespoons mayonnaise. Add 1 teaspoon paprika, 1 tablespoon sherry, and a little salt and pepper. Place in the pastry shells and garnish with small parsley sprigs.

Fruity Chicken
Finely dice $\frac{1}{4}$ lb. cooked chicken meat. Mix it with 2 tablespoons fruit chutney, such as mango or apricot. Add 1 tablespoon chopped pimento and 1 tablespoon mayonnaise; mix well. Stir in a few drops of chili sauce, and spoon the mixture into bouchée shells.

Ham and Egg Salad
Hard-boil three eggs; cool and remove the shells. Finely chop the egg and mix it with $\frac{1}{4}$ cup mayonnaise. Chop 2 oz. lean ham and three scallions and mix into the egg; season to taste. Spoon into the bouchée shells.

Caviar-Avocado
Cream the pulp of a large avocado with $\frac{1}{4}$ cup sour cream and a few drops of chili sauce. Spoon or pipe the mixture into the bouchée shells, and top with a teaspoonful of red or black caviar-style roe. Sprinkle a little lemon juice on top.

Anchovy Cream Cheese
Beat $\frac{2}{3}$ cup cream cheese with $\frac{1}{4}$ cup heavy cream. Stir in 1 tablespoon grated onion, a little salt and pepper, $\frac{1}{2}$ teaspoon paprika, and six finely chopped anchovy fillets. Spoon or pipe the mixture into the bouchée shells and sprinkle a dusting of paprika on top.

1111

Bass Melbourne

one 2-lb. bass or mullet
4 ozs. unflavored gelatin
¼ cup butter
½ lb. shrimp, cooked
1 lemon, sliced
1 cucumber, sliced
¼ sweet red pepper, seeded and
  chopped

For the Stock:
4¼ cups water
2¼ cups cider
⅔ cup tomato juice
1 tablespoon honey
1 large onion, cut in rings
1 carrot, sliced
1 clove garlic, crushed
1 branch celery, sliced
bouquet garni
salt and pepper

For the Sauce:
1 tablespoon butter
2 tablespoons flour
1 teaspoon prepared mustard
4 egg yolks
1¼ cups oil
pulp 1 avocado, mashed
½ small onion, chopped
1 tablespoon mixture of chopped
  parsley and coriander leaves

1 Place the ingredients for the stock in a large saucepan and boil for 10 minutes, stirring occasionally.

2 Tie up the fish to hold it in a figure 'S' shape and place it in a fish kettle. Cover with the stock and simmer for 20 minutes. Cool the fish in the stock. Remove the fish and peel off its skin. Strain and reserve 2¼ cups of the stock. Reheat half of this stock and dissolve the gelatin in it.

3 Brush the fish twice with a little of this aspic and pour the rest into the center of a large, shallow serving dish. Place the fish on top and leave in a cool place until set.

4 Beat the butter until light and fluffy and place it in a decorator's bag fitted with a plain nozzle. Pipe a rim of butter along the spine of the fish and decorate the head.

5 Peel the shrimp and reserve 8 heads. Flute the edges of the sliced lemon and halve each slice. Do the same with the cucumber slices.

6 Place the shrimp heads along the spine of the fish on top of the butter and arrange the shrimp on the aspic along either side of the fish. Decorate the side of the dish with lemon slices dotted with red pepper and the cucumber slices. Chill.

7 Prepare the sauce. Melt the butter in a pan and stir in the flour. Cook for 1 minute and gradually stir in the remaining fish stock. Allow to cool.

8 Place the mustard, egg yolks, salt and pepper in a bowl. Add the oil in a thin trickle, whisking continually until the sauce is emulsified and thick. Stir in the fish stock sauce, mashed avocado pulp, chopped onion, parsley and coriander. Check the seasoning and serve the Melbourne sauce separately.

Serves 6–8

Spiced Sirloin Sandringham

2 lbs. boned sirloin
salt and pepper
¼ cup oil
4 endive leaves
24 asparagus spears, cooked
2 slices red pepper

For the Glaze:
⅓ cup red currant jelly
1 tablespoon vinegar
juice 1 orange
1 teaspoon ground ginger
garlic salt
1 teaspoon mixed cinnamon and
  mace

1 Preheat the oven to 400°F. Sea-son the meat and rub it with oil. Roast it for 45 minutes. Cool.

2 Slice the beef and arrange the slices in overlapping layers on a large shallow dish.

3 Boil the ingredients for the glaze for 4 minutes, stirring continuously. Brush the cooled slices of meat 3 times with the glaze and let set.

4 Cut each endive leaf in two and place 3 asparagus spears in the hollow of each half. Cut the red pepper into 8 equal strips and place them over each asparagus basket. Chill and serve garnished with watercress.

Serves 6–8

Muscovite Salad

2 ozs. ham, cubed
2 ozs. tongue, cooked and cubed
½ cup cooked carrots, diced
½ cup canned corn, drained
½ cup cooked peas
½ cup cooked green beans, diced
2 small potatoes, boiled and cubed
1 sweet red pepper, seeded and
  chopped
salt and pepper
1¼ cups mayonnaise
2 ozs. anchovy fillets
drained capers for decoration

1 Place the ham, tongue, carrots, corn, peas, beans, potatoes and red pepper in a large salad bowl. Season and add the mayonnaise. Toss gently but thoroughly.

2 Arrange the anchovy fillets over the top in a lattice pattern and place a caper in the center of each diamond. Chill and serve.

Serves 8–10

*Spiced Sirloin Sandringham is
garnished with endive and
asparagus and served with a tasty
Muscovite Salad*

Orange Surprises

9 oranges
2 cups sponge cake, cubed
¼ cup orange liqueur
1¼ cups whipping cream
2 tablespoons sugar
candied angelica, chopped for
  decoration

1 Cut the tops off the oranges and scoop out the flesh; squeeze the juice and reserve. Place the sponge cake cubes inside the oranges. Sprinkle with liqueur and orange juice.

2 Whip the cream and sugar until stiff and pipe onto the oranges. Garnish with the orange tops and chopped angelica.

Serves 9

Lotus Blossom Chicken

one 3-lb. roasting chicken
salt and pepper
2 tablespoons butter
2 tablespoons oil

For the Glaze:
⅓ cup honey
1 tablespoon vinegar
1 tablespoon soy sauce

For the Aspic:
⅔ cup water
⅓ cup orange juice
2 tablespoons gelatin

Orange Surprises, topped with swirls of fresh cream and angelica 'leaves,' will make a juicy refreshing dessert

1 orange
3 black olives

For the Accompaniments:
6 pineapple slices
2 ozs. cream cheese
¼ cup heavy cream
6 black olives
1 cucumber
⅔ cup fruit chutney

1 Preheat the oven to 400°F. Sprinkle the chicken with salt and pepper and place in a roasting pan with the butter and oil. Roast for 45-60 minutes, basting from time to time.

2 To make the glaze: melt the honey, vinegar, and soy sauce in a pan. Cook for 5 minutes. Spread the glaze over the chicken. Replace the chicken in the oven and cook for 5-10 minutes. Cool.

3 To make the aspic: warm the water and orange juice and dissolve the gelatin in it. Brush the liquid over the cold chicken. Peel the orange and cut three slices. Dip them in the liquid and fasten them to breast of the chicken with toothpicks; top the ends of the toothpicks with black olives. Brush the remaining aspic liquid over the chicken. Leave in the refrigerator until set.

4 To make the accompaniments: arrange the pineapple slices on the serving dish around the chicken. Beat the cream cheese and cream together and spoon or pipe the mixture into the middle of the pineapple slices. Top each one with a black olive. Cut grooves along the cucumber with a zesting knife and cut the cucumber into 1½-inch chunks. Fill each one with fruit chutney. Arrange the cucumber pieces between the pineapple slices. Garnish with coriander leaves or parsley.

Serves 10–12

Lotus Blossom Chicken with its delicate Chinese flavor and a colorful garnish will delight your guests

Cucumber, Celery and Apple Salad

4 apples
1 cucumber
5 branches celery
⅔ cup plain yogurt
¼ cup mayonnaise
juice 1 lemon
coriander leaves for decoration

1 Peel, core and chop the apples. Make grooves lengthwise along the cucumber using a zesting knife, and slice thinly. Slice the celery.

2 Combine the yogurt, mayonnaise and lemon juice.

3 Mix the apples, cucumber and celery with the prepared dressing, then transfer to a serving dish and decorate with the coriander leaves.

Serves 8

Marzipan (almond paste)

Oranges
Color marzipan with a few drops of orange food coloring and shape into small balls. Roll them on a grater, and use a toothpick to mark

An assortment of marzipan fruits, frosted grapes and chocolate litchis are a tempting finish to a buffet

lines at the stalk end. Mark the 'stalk' with a spot of melted chocolate.

Bananas
Roll the marzipan into small sausages, taper the ends and bend slightly to form banana shapes. Mark the bananas with melted chocolate, using a toothpick.

Pears
Color some marzipan with green food coloring and form into pear shapes. Indent the stalk ends and insert a clove to represent a stalk. Using a fingertip, rub a little red food coloring on to each 'pear.'

Dates
Slit some fresh or dried dates along one side and remove the pit. Fill each with a sausage-shaped piece of marzipan.

Chocolate Litchis
Dip some peeled litchis into melted plain chocolate and leave on wax paper to set. When they are set, pipe a decoration of melted milk chocolate onto each. The pit may be removed from the litchi before dipping, if preferred, although this makes the process more difficult.

Grapes
Melt some sugar in a pan, then boil until it is a rich golden color. Remove from the heat and immediately dip small clusters of green grapes into it. Stand on wax paper to set.

Exotic Fruit Salad

The recipe below is for the perfect exotic fruit salad. If you are unable to find some of the fruits that have been specified, simply increase the quantity of another. Wash all the fruits carefully, then prepare them over a bowl so that all the juice is caught.

two, removing the membrane between the sections.

3 Slice the bananas and toss in the lemon juice, then place the bananas, lemon juice and orange sections in a large bowl with the prepared fruit, reserving a little for decoration.

4 Add the juice from the prepared fruit to the cold sugar syrup and strain it over the fruit. Arrange the reserved fruit decoratively on top.

Serves 18

Party Nibbles

Here are a few ideas for tasty party nibbles to serve with drinks.

Bell Ropes

Thinly roll out $\frac{3}{4}$ lb. prepared puff pastry and trim to a neat square. Spread with 1 tablespoon yeast and sprinkle on $\frac{1}{2}$ cup finely grated cheese. Fold in three, press down lightly and brush with beaten egg. Cut into $\frac{1}{4}$-inch fingers, twist them and place on a lightly greased baking sheet. Bake at 425°F. for 15-20 minutes.

Curried Nuts

Melt 2 tablespoons butter in a pan. Add $\frac{3}{4}$ cup mixed nuts and sauté for 3-4 minutes. Stir in a few shakes of onion salt and a good pinch of curry powder.

Confetti Popcorn

Prepare $\frac{1}{2}$ cup popcorn following the directions. Melt $\frac{1}{3}$ cup butter and pour it over the prepared popcorn with a few shakes of garlic salt and paprika. Serve warm.

Love Hearts

Sift $\frac{3}{4}$ cup flour and rub in $\frac{1}{3}$ cup butter. Add $\frac{3}{4}$ cup grated cheese, salt and pepper and 1 beaten egg. Roll out thinly, cut out heart shapes and sprinkle with sesame seeds or finely chopped walnuts. Place on a baking sheet lined with wax paper and bake at 375°F. for 10 minutes.

3 lemons
3 oranges
$\frac{1}{3}$ cup sugar
3 large bananas
1 small honeydew melon, peeled, seeded and cubed
1 pineapple, peeled, cored and cubed
2 large mangoes, peeled, seeded and cubed
1 small papaya, peeled, seeded and cubed
2 large grapefruit, peeled, sectioned, pith and membranes removed
$\frac{1}{4}$ lb. purple grapes, skinned and seeded
$\frac{1}{2}$ lb. strawberries, hulled
$\frac{2}{3}$ cup fresh dates, peeled, halved and seeded
8 kiwi fruit, peeled and cut into wedges

Exotic Fruit Salad probably contains many fruits you have never tasted so make this an opportunity to try them

$\frac{1}{4}$ lb. kumquats
$\frac{1}{2}$ lb. litchis
5 pieces candied ginger, chopped

1 Remove the peel from the lemons and oranges using a vegetable peeler, and place in a pan with the sugar and 2 cups of water. Stir over gentle heat until the sugar has dissolved, then bring to a boil and simmer gently for 3 minutes. Remove the pan from the heat and cool.

2 Squeeze the juice from the lemons. Slice one of the oranges for decoration and section the other

1117

Spanish Buffet

Our Spanish Buffet is designed for 12 people and offers a variety of hot and cold dishes. Your guests can choose between a warm tart and a chilled soup to start with, followed by a hot or cold chicken dish. Make two Almond Cheesecakes for dessert, and serve Spicy Pickled Olives to nibble with drinks.

Spicy Pickled Olives

thinly peeled rind 1 orange
one 10-oz. jar stuffed green olives
white vinegar
1 teaspoon pickling spice
2 tablespoons sugar
1 clove garlic, crushed

1 Cut the orange peel into strips.

2 Drain the brine from the jar of olives into a measuring cup. Place double this quantity of vinegar in a saucepan with the orange strips, spice, sugar and garlic, bring to a boil and simmer for 3 minutes. The brine will not be needed.

3 Remove from the heat and allow to cool completely.

4 Pour the cold vinegar mixture into the jar of olives, cover and refrigerate for at least 24 hours. These Spicy Pickled Olives will keep in the refrigerator for up to 1 month.

Makes 10 ozs.

Spanish Summer Soup

½ cucumber, chopped
½ green pepper, seeded
1 onion, peeled and chopped
8 radishes, chopped
stalks from 1 bunch watercress
1 clove garlic, crushed
3 tablespoons oil
1 tablespoon Worcestershire sauce
5 cups tomato juice
pepper to taste

To Garnish:
1 small green pepper, seeded and diced
1 small sweet red pepper, seeded and diced
¼ cucumber, diced
1 small onion, diced
3 tomatoes, seeded and diced
10 radishes, diced
3 branches celery, diced
2 slices bread, toasted and diced

1 Place all the soup ingredients in an electric blender and blend until smooth. Chill thoroughly.

2 Serve the soup surrounded with small piles of the diced garnish ingredients.

Serves 9

Sherried Chicken

6 chicken pieces
¼ cup butter
3 tablespoons oil
2 onions, peeled and finely chopped
1 clove garlic, crushed
3 tablespoons flour
⅔ cup dry sherry
1¼ cups chicken stock
6 tomatoes, skinned and chopped
salt and pepper
¼ cup sliced cooked ham

1 Remove the skin from the chicken pieces. Heat the butter and oil in a skillet and sauté the onions, garlic and chicken until lightly golden.

2 Sprinkle the flour into the pan and cook, stirring, until the flour is absorbed and lightly browned. Gradually stir in the sherry and stock and bring to a boil. Add the tomatoes and seasoning, cover and simmer very gently for 50-60 minutes.

3 Cut the cooked ham into strips and stir into the chicken mixture.

4 Serve the chicken hot, with peas and boiled potatoes sprinkled with parsley.

Serves 6

Almond Cheesecake

shortening for greasing
4 ozs. cream cheese
½ cup sugar
⅔ cup ground almonds
4 eggs, separated
finely grated rind and juice 1 lemon
2 tablespoons flour
1 teaspoon almond extract
2 tablespoons sliced almonds

1 Preheat the oven to 450°F. Grease an 8-inch cake pan.

2 Blend the cream cheese in a bowl with the sugar, ground almonds, egg yolks, lemon rind and juice, flour and almond extract.

3 Beat the egg whites until stiff and fold into the mixture. Turn into the prepared pan and bake for 30 minutes.

4 Remove the pan from the oven and top the cheesecake with the sliced almonds. Reduce the oven temperature to 350°F. and bake for a further 30 minutes. Cool in the pan.

Serves 6–8

Start your Spanish Buffet with Spicy Pickled Olives and Spanish Summer Soup, followed by Pamplona Pilaf, Sherried Chicken and Almond Cheesecake

Spanish Leek Tart

2¼ cups flour
pinch salt
⅞ cup butter
2 tablespoons oil
¼ lb. smoked bacon slices, chopped
½ lb. cooked ham, diced
6 leeks, thickly sliced
1 cup chicken stock
salt and pepper
4 eggs, beaten

1 Sift the flour and salt into a bowl and rub in the butter. Work it into a ball, wrap and chill for 1 hour.

2 Heat the oil in a skillet and fry the bacon and ham until lightly golden. Add the leeks and cook gently for 10 minutes, stirring constantly.

3 Add the stock and seasoning, and cook gently for 45 minutes. Remove from the heat, cool, then stir in the beaten eggs.

4 Preheat the oven to 400°F. Press the pastry into a 9-inch fluted flan pan, and prick the base with a fork. Bake for 10 minutes. Spoon in the prepared filling, reduce the oven temperature to 375°F. and bake the tart for a further 30-35 minutes. Serve warm.

Serves 6

Spanish Leek Tart has an especially rich, buttery pastry crust and is filled with a mixture of ham, leeks and bacon

Pamplona Pilaf

¼ teaspoon powdered saffron
1 tablespoon lemon juice
¾ cup long-grain rice
6 chicken pieces
3 tablespoons flour seasoned with salt
¼ cup butter
1 tablespoon oil
4 large zucchini, sliced
1 sweet red pepper, cut into strips

10 stuffed olives
¼ lb. sliced cooked ham
salt and pepper

To Garnish:
8 cooked mussels
8 whole cooked, peeled, deveined shrimp
2 tablespoons tomato paste

1 Place the saffron and lemon juice together in a small bowl. Cook the rice in boiling salted water for 15-20 minutes until tender. Drain, stir in the saffron and lemon juice, then cool.

2 Lightly coat the chicken pieces with the seasoned flour. Heat the butter and oil in a skillet and sauté the zucchini and pepper until soft. Remove with a slotted spoon.

3 Add the chicken pieces to the pan, skin-side up, and fry until golden. Turn the chicken over, cover the pan and fry gently for 20-30 minutes, turning twice. Remove the cooked chicken from the pan and allow to cool.

4 Slice half of the olives and cut the sliced ham into strips. Combine all the pilaf ingredients, turn into a serving dish and garnish with the mussels, shrimp and a teaspoon of the tomato paste.

Serves 6

Entertaining: Memorable Meals

Hawaiian Chicken

Menu

Broccoli au Gratin

★

Chicken Juliette

★

Raspberry Sherbert Surprise

★

Almond Biscuits

Broccoli au Gratin

¼ lb. broccoli florets
4 large slices cooked ham
2 tablespoons butter
3 tablespoons flour
1¾ cups milk
¾ cup grated cheese
salt and pepper

1 Preheat the oven to 400°F.

2 Cook the broccoli in boiling salted water for 5 minutes, drain and divide between the slices of ham. Roll them up and arrange in a shallow ovenproof dish.

3 Melt the butter, stir in the flour and cook for 1 or 2 minutes. Gradually add the milk, bring to a boil and simmer for 2 or 3 minutes, stirring continuously. Add ½ cup of the cheese, season to taste and pour the sauce over the ham rolls.

4 Sprinkle the remaining cheese over the top and bake for 25-35 minutes. Serve immediately.

Serves 4

Chicken Juliette

1 orange
2 tablespoons butter
1 tablespoon oil

1 onion, peeled and sliced
4 chicken pieces
½ cup flour seasoned with salt
2¼ cups chicken stock
⅔ cup white wine
1 tablespoon Worcestershire sauce
⅓ cup raisins
sprigs of watercress

1 Preheat the oven to 350°F. Thinly pare the orange rind and cut it into thin strips. Squeeze the juice.

2 Heat the butter and oil and sauté the onion gently until soft but not browned. Remove with a slotted spoon and place in an ovenproof casserole.

3 Toss the chicken in the seasoned flour, and fry until evenly browned. Add to the casserole with the stock, wine, Worcestershire sauce, orange strips and juice and raisins.

4 Cover the casserole and cook in the preheated oven for 1 hour.

5 Transfer to a heated serving dish and garnish with sprigs of watercress. Serve with cauliflower.

Serves 4

Raspberry Sherbet Surprise

¼ cup sugar
1¼ cups water
¾ lb. frozen raspberries, thawed
juice ½ lemon
2 egg whites
frozen and thawed raspberries to decorate

1 Dissolve the sugar in the water in a pan. Bring to a boil, simmer for 10 minutes, then cool.

2 Strain the raspberries and add half of the purée to the cooled sugar syrup with the lemon juice. Pour into a 1-quart bowl and place in the freezer until it begins to thicken.

3 Beat the egg whites until stiff and

fold lightly into the thickened mixture. Place an empty sour cream or yogurt container in the center and hold it in place with a weight, so that the sherbet freezes evenly around the sides of the bowl. Freeze until firm.

4 Remove the container from the center of the sherbert and fill the hole with the remaining raspberry purée. Refreeze until firm.

5 Thirty minutes before serving, place the sherbet in the refrigerator to soften. Turn out onto a chilled serving plate and decorate with the whole raspberries. Serve with Almond Tuile Cookies.

Serves 6

Almond Tuile Cookies

⅓ cup butter
⅓ cup sugar
½ cup flour
pinch salt
½ cup almonds, finely chopped

1 Preheat the oven to 400°F.

2 Cream the butter and sugar until light and fluffy. Sift the flour and salt and stir into the creamed mixture with the almonds.

3 Place a teaspoonful of the mixture on a well-greased baking sheet and flatten with a wet fork. Repeat with 3 more teaspoonfuls and bake for 6-8 minutes until lightly colored. Allow to stand for a second or two, then remove with a sharp knife and curl on a rolling pin until set.

4 Repeat the process until all of the mixture is used up.

Makes about 12

Broccoli au Gratin, Chicken Juliette, Raspberry Sherbet Surprise and Almond Tuile Cookies make a fine meal

Menu

Tangy Carrot Soup

★

Prussian Beef Casserole

★

Sweet Cardamom Potatoes

★

Blackberry and Apple Compote

Tangy Carrot Soup

2 tablespoons olive oil
1 onion, sliced
1 lb. carrots, peeled and diced
3 cups strong chicken stock
juice and grated rind 1 orange
2 bay leaves
bouquet garni
salt and pepper
2 tablespoons sour cream
1 tablespoon chopped chives

1 Heat the oil in a saucepan. Add the onion and carrot and cook over high heat until the onion is transparent and the oil has been completely absorbed.

2 Add the stock, orange juice, grated orange rind, bay leaves and bouquet garni. Season.

3 Bring the soup mixture to a boil. Cover and simmer for 30 minutes or until the carrots are tender.

4 Remove the bay leaves and bouquet garni and purée the soup to a smooth consistency, either by forcing it through a strainer or using a blender.

5 Reheat the soup and check the seasoning. Pour it into 4 warm bowls and serve each one with a dollop of sour cream and a sprinkling of chopped chives.

Serves 4

Prussian Beef Casserole

2 lbs. stewing beef, cut into cubes
½ cup flour seasoned with salt and pepper
¼ cup butter
2 tablespoons oil
½ lb. baby carrots, peeled
½ lb. shallots, peeled
2 cloves garlic crushed
½ bunch celery, chopped
1¼ cups beef stock
⅔ cup dry red wine
1 tablespoon mixed rosemary and thyme
1 teaspoon chopped parsley

1 Preheat the oven to 350°F. Roll the meat in the seasoned flour. Heat the butter and oil in a large skillet, add the meat and brown it on all sides. Reserve the remaining flour. Transfer the browned meat to an ovenproof casserole.

2 Add the carrots, shallots and garlic to the pan and brown slightly. Transfer them to the casserole with the chopped celery.

3 Add enough of the reserved seasoned flour to the oil in the pan to make a paste, and stir over gentle heat for 1 minute. Gradually stir in the stock, red wine and mixed herbs and cook gently, stirring continually, until the sauce thickens. Check the seasoning and pour it over the meat in the casserole.

4 Cover and cook the casserole in the oven for 1–1½ hours or until the meat is tender. Garnish with chopped parsley and serve with a dish of Sweet Cardamom Potatoes and a crisp green salad.

Serves 4

Sweet Cardamom Potatoes

3 medium-size potatoes
juice and finely grated rind 1 orange
1 tablespoon honey
1 onion, thinly sliced
salt
2 teaspoons ground cardamom
¼ cup butter
2 tablespoons fresh breadcrumbs

1 Preheat the oven to 375°F.

2 Wash and peel the potatoes and slice them thinly. In a bowl, mix together the orange juice, grated orange rind and honey.

3 Arrange the potato slices and onion rings in alternate layers in a well-greased ovenproof dish. Pour on the orange and honey mixture and sprinkle with salt and the ground cardamom. Dot with butter and sprinkle with the fresh breadcrumbs. Bake uncovered in the oven for 45 minutes and serve immediately.

Serves 4

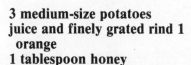

Blackberry and Apple Compote

 ★ ☰☰

shortcake made with 2¼ cups flour
2 tart apples, peeled, cored and sliced
1½ cups blackberries
½ cup sugar

1 Grease a 1-quart pudding bowl and line it with ¾ of the shortcake.

2 Carefully mix the apple slices and blackberries. Fill the bowl with layers of fruit, sprinkling with sugar between each layer. Cover with the remaining shortcake and seal the edges.

3 Cover the basin with aluminum foil and steam in a double boiler for 2 hours. Turn the pudding out onto a warm serving dish and serve with a bowl of whipped cream.

Serves 4

Tangy Carrot Soup and Prussian Beef Casserole, followed by Blackberry and Apple Compote, makes a superb meal

Menu

Tomato Soup *or* Fish
and Herb Pancakes

★

Stuffed Roast Lamb

★

Stuffed Onions

★

Cheeseboard

Fish and Herb Pancakes

½ lb. white fish fillets
a little milk
¼ lb. cooked shrimp, peeled and
  deveined
2 tablespoons butter
¼ cup flour
1¼ cups milk
2 tablespoons chopped fennel bulb
pinch dill
few drops anchovy paste
salt and cayenne pepper
parsley to garnish

For the Pancakes:
1 cup + 2 tablespoons flour
pinch salt
1 egg
1¼ cups milk
1 tablespoon melted butter
a little oil

1 Make the pancakes: sift the flour and salt into a bowl. Add the egg and milk and beat to a smooth batter. Add the butter and beat again. Heat a little oil in a pan and make 8 pancakes. Keep them warm.

2 Poach the fish in a little milk for 5 minutes, or until tender. Drain the fish, reserving the poaching liquid. Flake and mix with the shrimp.

3 Melt the butter in a pan and stir in the flour. Cook for 1-2 minutes, stirring continually. Gradually blend in the reserved poaching liquid and, if necessary, add enough milk to make it up to 1¾

cups. Stir over gentle heat until it thickens. Add the fish, shrimp, fennel, dill and anchovy paste and stir well. Season.

4 Divide the mixture among the pancakes and fold each in half and then quarters. Serve garnished with parsley.

Serves 8

Stuffed Roast Lamb with Mint Sauce

¼ cup butter
1 onion, peeled and chopped
2 cups fresh breadcrumbs
1 tablespoon rosemary
1 tablespoon thyme
1 egg, beaten
salt and pepper
one 4-lb. rolled loin of lamb
2 tablespoons melted butter
3 tablespoons white wine

For the Sauce:
handful mint leaves, finely
  chopped
1 tablespoon sugar
2 tablespoons boiling water
3 tablespoons dry white wine
pinch salt
1 teaspoon cornstarch

1 Melt the butter and sauté the onion until soft. In a bowl, mix the onion, breadcrumbs and herbs, adding enough beaten egg to bind. Season and spread over the lamb. Roll up the loin and secure with string.

2 Place the lamb in a roasting pan with the melted butter and wine and bake for 1½-2 hours, basting frequently, until cooked.

3 Mix the mint and sugar and pour in the boiling water. Add the wine and salt and mix well.

4 Place the cooked lamb on a serving dish and keep warm. Combine the juices in the roasting pan with the sauce. Pour into a pan and add the cornstarch blended with a little

water. Stir continually over gentle heat until thickened. Serve the lamb, garnished with parsley, with the sauce stuffed onions and buttered carrots.

Serves 8

Stuffed Onions

8 large onions, skinned
1¼ cups chicken stock
pinch marjoram
salt and pepper
3 tablespoons flour
¼ cup light cream

For the Stuffing:
3 cups breadcrumbs
4 tomatoes, peeled and chopped
½ cup black olives, pitted
1 egg, beaten

1 Place the onions, stock, marjoram and seasoning in a saucepan and poach for about 10 minutes. Remove the onions and reserve the stock.

2 Scoop out the onion centers and chop. Mix the stuffing ingredients with the onion, adding sufficient beaten egg to bind it together. Fill the onion shells with the mixture and place them in a roasting bag in a roasting pan. Bake for 15-20 minutes.

3 Place the stock in a saucepan and heat gently. Add the flour and stir until the sauce thickens. Stir in the cream and serve poured over the onions. Garnish with chopped herbs.

Serves 8

---

*Tomato Soup, Stuffed Onions,
Fish and Herb Pancakes, with a
Stuffed Roast of Lamb with mint
sauce — quite a meal!*

Menu

Iced Avocado Soup
★
Chicken Lavandou
★
Creamed Potatoes
★
**Strawberries in
Orange Juice**

Iced Avocado Soup

3 ripe avocados, peeled, pitted
  and mashed
juice $\frac{1}{2}$ lemon
salt and pepper
$1\frac{1}{4}$ cups chicken stock
toasted croûtons to garnish

1 Mix the avocado, lemon juice, and seasoning with enough stock to give a smooth consistency. Chill well.

2 Serve garnished with crisp croûtons.

Serves 4

Chicken Lavandou

$\frac{1}{3}$ cup butter
$\frac{1}{4}$ lb. thick smoked bacon slices
4 chicken pieces
1 onion, peeled and finely
  chopped
4 shallots, peeled and finely
  chopped
1 carrot, peeled and finely diced
1 tablespoon flour
$1\frac{1}{4}$ cups dry white wine
$\frac{1}{4}$ cup tomato paste
$\frac{1}{4}$ teaspoon fennel seeds
salt and pepper
$\frac{1}{2}$ lb. mushrooms, washed
  and trimmed
1 cup green olives, pitted

1 Melt $\frac{1}{4}$ cup of the butter in a large pan, add the bacon and fry until golden. Remove from the pan with a slotted spoon. Add the chicken pieces to the pan, fry until golden and remove from the pan.

2 Sauté the onion, shallot and carrot until golden. Stir in the flour and cook for 2 minutes, then gradually add the wine, tomato paste, fennel seeds and seasoning

---

Iced Avocado Soup is ideal for summer menus, but its smooth creamy texture and delicate flavor are welcome at any time

---

and cook gently for 15 minutes.

3 Add the chicken pieces to the pan, cover and simmer for 30 minutes.

4 Meanwhile, heat the remaining butter in a small pan and sauté the mushrooms for 3 or 4 minutes. Remove from the pan and drain on absorbent paper.

5 Place the olives in a pan with cold water to cover, bring to a boil and simmer for 5 minutes. Drain and rinse in cold water.

6 Remove the cooked chicken pieces from the pan, and purée or strain the sauce. Return the sauce to the pan with the chicken, bacon, mushrooms and olives and cook gently for 10 minutes to heat through.

7 Transfer the chicken and sauce to a heated serving dish. Serve very hot, with creamed potatoes and a fresh green vegetable.

Serves 4

Strawberries in Orange Juice

8 sugar cubes
1 large orange
$\frac{1}{4}$ cup brandy
1 lb. strawberries, hulled

1 Rub the sugar cubes over the orange rind until they are soaked with oil. Crush them with the juice from the orange, then add the brandy.

2 Place the strawberries in a serving bowl and pour on the orange mixture. Cover and chill for 3 hours before serving.

Serves 4

Chicken Lavandou, with a sauce containing bacon, olives and mushrooms, brings a taste of France to your table

Menu

**Chilled Celery
Starter** *or*
Pumpkin Soup

★

Roast Beef

★

Brandy Mince Tart

★

**Cinnamon Cherries
in Wine**

Chilled Celery Starter

8 branches celery
2 cups mushrooms
2 teaspoons paprika
2 teaspoons curry powder
$\frac{1}{3}$ cup olive oil
3 tablespoons lemon juice
salt and pepper
$\frac{1}{2}$ lb. peeled shrimp
2 tablespoons chopped parsley

1 Cut the celery into 1-inch lengths. Slice the mushrooms and mix them in a bowl with the celery. Mix the paprika and curry powder with the olive oil. Add the lemon juice, seasoning, shrimp, and chopped parsley.

2 Pour the oil sauce over the celery and mushrooms. Toss well and chill before serving.

Serves 8

Pumpkin Soup

$\frac{1}{4}$ cup butter
1 large white onion, finely
  chopped
2$\frac{1}{4}$ cups chicken stock
1 lb. fresh pumpkin

2$\frac{1}{4}$ cups hot milk
pinch grated nutmeg
salt and pepper
croûtons for garnish

1 Melt the butter in a large saucepan and gently sauté the onion for 10 minutes, or until soft. Add the chicken stock and bring it to a boil.

2 Peel the pumpkin and cut it into 2-inch chunks. Add it to the stock and simmer for about 30 minutes or until tender. Cool. Work the pumpkin and stock through a strainer, or purée it in an electric blender.

3 Return to the pan, add the hot milk, nutmeg and seasoning and heat gently. Serve in a tureen garnished with croûtons.

Serves 8

Tip: This soup is quite delicious served with a little sour cream and chopped chives. You can make pumpkin and turnip soup by substituting $\frac{1}{2}$ lb. of turnips for half of the pumpkin and preparing it in the same way.

Roast Ribs of Beef with Potatoes and Celery

4-lbs. rib of beef
$\frac{1}{4}$ cup softened butter
salt and pepper
9 medium-size potatoes, peeled
$\frac{1}{2}$ cup flour
lard or meat drippings
2 bunches celery
2 tablespoons butter
1$\frac{1}{4}$ cups stock
watercress

1 Preheat the oven to 350°F.

2 Rub the meat all over with the softened butter. Season to taste and place in a large roasting bag. Tie the bag, according to the instructions, and roast the meat in a roasting pan for 1$\frac{1}{2}$ hours or until tender.

3 When the meat has been in the oven for $\frac{1}{2}$ hour, prepare the potatoes. Cut them into equal-sized

pieces and parboil them in salted water for 5 minutes. Drain and dry them before sprinkling with a little of the flour. Place them in a clean roasting dish with the meat or drippings and bake them for the last hour of the meat's cooking time.

4 Wash and peel the celery and cut off the tops, leaving 6-8 inches of heart. Remove the outer leaves, then cut the hearts in half, or into three if they are large. Sprinkle them with seasoning and place them in a roasting bag with the butter, cut into pats. Tie the bag according to instructions and place it in the roasting pan with the meat for the last 45 minutes of the meat's cooking time.

5 When the meat and vegetables are ready, reduce the heat and leave the potatoes in the oven to keep warm. Remove the meat and celery from the roasting bags, reserving the juices. Place the meat on a serving dish and the celery in a vegetable dish. Keep them warm. Make the gravy: place the reserved juices in the roasting tray. Blend them with the remaining flour and cook over gentle heat until it bubbles. Add the stock and bring to a boil, stirring constantly. If it is too pale, add a little gravy coloring. Serve the meat garnished with watercress and surrounded by the roasted potatoes and celery hearts. Serve the gravy separately.

Serves 8–9

Brandy Mince Tart

one 9-inch pie crust
$\frac{3}{4}$ cup mincemeat
1 large cooking apple, peeled and
  cored
juice 1 lemon
$\frac{1}{4}$ cup apricot jam
1 tablespoon brandy
2 teaspoons water

1 Preheat the oven to 375°F. Roll out the pastry to a thickness of $\frac{1}{4}$ inch and use it to line a 9-inch fluted ring set on a baking sheet. Trim the edges and spread the pastry with the mincemeat. Bake for 20 minutes, or until crisp and golden. Remove from the oven.

2 Cut the apple into even-sized slices and sprinkle them with the lemon juice. Arrange the slices in an overlapping ring around the edge of the mincemeat.

3 In a pan, stir the jam, brandy and water over gentle heat until well combined. Strain and brush over the tart. Bake for a further 15-20 minutes, and serve hot or cold, with whipped cream and brandy hard sauce.

Serves 8

Tip: To make brandy hard sauce, cream $\frac{1}{2}$ cup each of unsalted butter

Pumpkin Soup, Chilled Celery Starter and juicy Roast Ribs of Beef are followed by a delicious Brandy Mince Tart

and sugar until white. Beat in 2-3 tablespoons brandy, 1 teaspoon at a time. Chill until firm.

Cinnamon Cherries in Wine

2 lbs. fresh cherries
1¼ cups water
¾ cup sugar
1¼ cups dry red wine

2 tablespoons red currant jelly
small piece cinnamon stick

1 Discard the cherry stems and, if you prefer, remove the pits with a cherry stoner.

2 Place the water, sugar, wine, red currant jelly and cinnamon stick in a saucepan and bring to a boil.

3 Add the cherries and return to a boil. Reduce the heat and simmer uncovered for about 10 minutes.

4 Use a slotted spoon to transfer the cherries to a serving dish.

5 Bring the syrup to a boil and boil rapidly for a few minutes to reduce it a little. Strain the syrup over the cherries and cool slightly. Serve warm, not hot or cold, with a bowl of whipped cream.

Serves 8

Menu

Peach and Melon Boats

★

Halibut Minerva

★

Leaf Spinach

★

Chocolate Mousse

Peach and Melon Boats

1 small honeydew melon
6 canned peach halves
2 tablespoons syrup from canned peaches
2 tablespoons white port
8 cocktail cherries

1 Cut the melon into quarters and remove the seeds. Run a sharp knife carefully along the base of each quarter to cut away the flesh from the rind. Slice the melon across and position the slices to left and right alternately, overlapping the base, to resemble oars.

2 Dice two of the canned peach halves and sprinkle over each melon quarter. Pour on the peach syrup and port.

3 Place a peach half on each melon portion. Skewer 2 cocktail cherries on each of 4 toothpicks and use to secure each peach. Chill and serve.

Serves 4

Halibut Minerva

½ lb. fish bones and trimmings
1 onion, sliced
bouquet garni

⅔ cup water
⅔ cup dry white vermouth
salt and pepper
four 6-oz. halibut fillets
2 tablespoons butter
⅔ cup sliced mushrooms
¼ lb. green seedless grapes, skinned and deseeded
2 tablespoons flour
1 egg yolk
⅔ cup light cream
juice ½ lemon
pinch cayenne pepper
5 medium-size potatoes, cooked and mashed
milk and butter for creaming potatoes
1 egg, beaten
¼ lb. lobster tail, cut in chunks

1 Place the fish bones and trimmings, onion, bouquet garni, water, vermouth and seasoning in a saucepan. Bring to a boil and and boil for 20 minutes, then strain and cool.

2 Preheat the oven to 400°F. Wash and dry the fillets. Use half of the butter to grease a shallow ovenproof dish. Place the fish, mushrooms and grapes in the dish and cover with the fish stock. Cover the dish and bake in the oven for 20-25 minutes.

3 Remove the fish, mushrooms and grapes and keep warm, and reserve the cooking liquor.

4 Heat the remaining butter in a small pan and add the flour. Cook for 2-3 minutes without browning. Then gradually add the reserved fish liquor, stirring all the time until you have a smooth sauce.

5 In a small bowl, blend the egg yolk and cream and stir in half of the sauce. Blend well, then pour back into the pan. Reheat the sauce — be careful not to let it boil. Season and stir in the lemon juice and cayenne pepper.

6 Blend the mashed potato with a little milk and butter. Pipe a border of creamed potato around the border of a shallow ovenproof dish and brush with beaten egg. Arrange the fish, mushrooms, grapes and lobster tail inside the dish and cover with the sauce. Place the dish under a hot broiler for 5 minutes to

brown the potato border and glaze the sauce. Serve with leaf spinach.

Serves 4

Tip: You may wish to substitute sole or flounder in this delicious dish.

Chocolate Mousse

8 ozs. semi-sweet chocolate
3 tablespoons black coffee
1 tablespoon butter
1 tablespoon orange-flavored liqueur
3 large eggs, separated

1 Break the chocolate into small pieces. Place the chocolate and black coffee in a small bowl standing over a pan of hot water over gentle heat. Stir continually until the chocolate melts and becomes creamy. Cook gently for 2-3 minutes.

2 Remove the bowl and stir in the butter and liqueur. Cool slightly before beating in the egg yolks.

3 Beat the egg whites until stiff and fold into the chocolate mixture. Spoon into glasses or individual dishes and chill in the refrigerator until set (about 1 hour). Serve decorated with a swirl of whipped cream and ladyfingers.

Serves 4

Tip: This mousse is very rich and you will find that a little goes a long way. It looks very attractive when served in small china pots and can be stretched to serve 6 people.

Peach and Melon Boats, Halibut Minerva and Chocolate Mousse all combine to make a satisfying dinner

Menu

Haddock Delight
★
Cornish Hens Basquaise
★
Creamed Potatoes
★
**Fresh Fruit and
Cheeseboard**

Haddock Delight

1 cup water
1 onion, chopped
bouquet garni
6 peppercorns
1 lb. smoked haddock
pinch salt
2 eggs, separated
2 lemons
1¼ cups aspic made with the
   cooking liquid and gelatin
⅔ cup heavy cream
½ cucumber, thinly sliced

1 Place the water in a pan with the onion, bouquet garni, peppercorns, smoked haddock and salt. Bring to a boil and poach the fish for about 10 minutes until it is cooked. Discard the bouquet garni and peppercorns and strain the fish from the liquid. Reserve the liquid.

2 Flake the fish in a bowl; discard any skin or bones. In another bowl, beat the egg yolks with the juice of half a lemon; stir in the aspic, made to the requested quantity with the cooking liquid and extra water. Stir this mixture into the fish; cool.

3 Beat the egg whites until stiff. Whip the cream until stiff and fold it into the egg whites. Fold this mixture into the fish.

4 Arrange halved cucumber slices in a lightly greased mold and pour the mixture over them. Refrigerate until set. Cut the other lemon in halved thin slices. Turn the mold out on a dish and decorate with lemon and cucumber slices.

Serves 6

---

*Haddock Delight is an attractive
color, complemented by a lemon
and cucumber border, and it
tastes delicious*

Cornish Hens Basquaise

two Cornish hens, about 2½ lbs.
¼ cup flour seasoned with salt and
   pepper
¼ cup oil
1 onion, sliced
½ cup sliced mushrooms
1 sweet red and 1 green pepper,
   seeded and diced
⅔ cup dry red wine
1¼ cups stock
1 tablespoon tomato paste
salt and pepper
pinch ground mace
1 tablespoon cornstarch
⅓ cup water

1 Cut the hens into pieces: drumsticks, thighs and breasts. Coat them with seasoned flour and fry them in the oil for 5 minutes until golden brown. Place in a casserole dish.

2 Sauté the onion in the same oil until golden. Add the mushrooms and peppers and sauté for a few minutes. Pour in the wine, bring to a boil and simmer for 5 minutes. Preheat the oven to 350°F.

3 Add the stock, tomato paste, seasoning and mace to the pan. Bring to a boil; turn down the heat. Stir the cornstarch into the water and add to the pan.

4 Pour the mixture over the pieces in the casserole, cover, and cook in the oven for 45 minutes to 1 hour until the hens are very tender. Transfer the hens and sauce to a heated serving dish and serve with creamed potatoes.

Serves 6

Tip: The dish will taste much better if a reasonably good wine rather than a very cheap one is used.

---

*Cornish Hens Basquaise, in a
richly flavored sauce with green
and red peppers, would be an
excellent family dish*

Look 'n Cook Cornish Hens Basquaise

1 Cut the hens into pieces — drumsticks, thighs and breasts 2 Dip the pieces into flour seasoned with salt and pepper; shake off the excess 3 Heat the oil in a skillet and fry the pieces until golden brown. Transfer them to a casserole dish 4 In the same oil, sauté the onion until golden. Add the mushrooms and peppers 5 Pour in the red wine and simmer for 5 minutes 6 Add the stock, tomato paste, seasoning and mace.

Bring to a boil, then reduce to a simmer **7** Add the diluted cornstarch **8** Pour the mixture into the casserole dish to cover the pieces. Cook in the preheated oven for 45 minutes to 1 hour, until the pieces are very tender **9** Transfer the pieces to a heated serving dish, covering them with the vegetable sauce **10** Serve at once

Menu

Fresh Melon

★

Spicy Turkey with
Beans

★

Green Salad

★

Baklava

Spicy Turkey with Beans

2 turkey breasts
¼ cup flour
2 tablespoons oil
1¼ cups plain yogurt
2 teaspoons tomato paste
1 teaspoon mixed allspice and
  mace
½ teaspoon ground nutmeg
1 teaspoon paprika
salt and black pepper
1 teaspoon Worcestershire sauce
1 lb. canned red kidney beans,
  rinsed and drained

1 Preheat the oven to 325°F.

2 Coat the turkey in the flour. Heat the oil in a skillet and brown the turkey quickly until golden on both sides. Transfer to a casserole dish.

3 Combine the yogurt with the tomato paste, spices, seasoning and Worcestershire sauce and pour over the turkey. Bake for 1 hour.

4 Heat the beans and place them in a heated serving dish. Place the turkey on top and pour on the sauce. Garnish with chopped parsley and lemon. Serve with hot garlic bread and salad.

Serves 4

Baklava

1 box filo (Greek pastry sheets)

Baklava, an eastern Mediterranean specialty, is rich with nuts and honey which make it an irresistible dessert

¼ lb. butter
melted butter for brushing

For the Filling:
⅓ cup unsalted butter, softened
⅔ cup each: finely chopped walnuts,
  almonds and pistachio nuts
2 tablespoons sugar
1 teaspoon cinnamon
pinch ground cloves
1 teaspoon lemon juice
1 teaspoon orange flower water

For the Syrup:
½ cup honey
1 cup water
2 whole cloves
1 stick cinnamon
2 teaspoons lemon juice
1 strip thinly pared lemon rind
1 teaspoon orange flower water

1 Preheat the oven to 425°F. Mix the filling ingredients to form a thick paste. Brush each of 10 folded filo sheets with butter. Spread with the filling. Brush each of 10 more filo sheets with butter, fold and place on top. Cut into triangles (see picture). Place on a non-stick baking sheet. Sprinkle with water.

2 Bake for 15 minutes, reduce the oven temperature to 325°F. and bake for a further 15-20 minutes, until well-risen and golden brown.

3 Meanwhile, heat all the syrup ingredients in a pan and simmer for 10 minutes. Strain and cool, then pour over the cooked baklava and leave for a few hours to soak. Serve cold.

Makes approximately 10

Spicy Turkey with Beans, an unusual but effective mixture of flavors and colors, is sure to please all the family

Menu

Figs in Parma Ham *or*
Vegetable Fondue

★

Duck Italian-style

★

Green Salad

★

Pineapple Cream

Figs in Parma Ham

8 lettuce leaves
8 figs, quartered
8 slices **Parma (prosciutto) ham**
watercress for garnishing

1 Arrange the lettuce leaves on 8 serving plates.

2 Wrap 4 fig quarters in each slice of ham and place each on a lettuce leaf. Garnish each dish with a little watercress and serve immediately.

Serves 8

Vegetable Fondue

This fondue is a famous specialty of the Piedmont region of Italy. In the country of its origin it is called Bagno Caldo which means 'hot bath.' It is a traditional Christmas Eve delicacy but we think it makes an exciting and novel appetizer.

1¼ **cups olive oil**
3 **cloves garlic, sliced**
½ **teaspoon freshly ground black pepper**
¼ **lb. canned anchovy fillets**

For the Dipping Vegetables:
sliced carrots
radishes
celery sticks
scallions
endive leaves

1 Heat the oil in a fondue pot with the garlic and pepper. Drain the anchovy fillets, reserving the oil. Chop the fillets and add them to the oil with the reserved anchovy oil. Heat until the oil is bubbling.

Pineapple Cream is a rich and creamy dessert with a velvety smooth texture, decorated with cherries and angelica

2 Arrange the fresh vegetables in a serving bowl, remembering to put toothpicks in the radishes. Allow each guest to dip his or her own vegetables in the oil.

Serves 8

Duck Italian-style

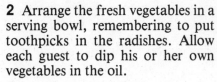

2 **small ducks**
¼ **cup butter**
¼ **cup oil**
2 **large onions, chopped**
2 **carrots, sliced**
2 **branches celery, chopped**
¼ **lb. bacon, sliced**
6 **tomatoes, peeled, seeded and chopped**
1¼ **cups chicken stock**
⅔ **cup dry white wine**
pinch basil
pinch sage
1 **teaspoon parsley**
salt and pepper
4 **cups ribbon pasta**
⅓ **cup grated Parmesan cheese**
2 **teaspoons cornstarch**

1 Cut each duck into 4 pieces. Heat half of the butter and the oil in a large skillet. Add the duck pieces, cover and brown on both sides for 10 minutes. Transfer the browned duck to a large ovenproof casserole.

2 Add the onions to the pan and sauté them gently until transparent. Add the carrots and celery and stir-fry for a further 5 minutes until lightly browned. Transfer all the vegetables to the casserole and discard the fat in the pan.

3 Add the bacon to the casserole with the chopped tomatoes, chicken stock and wine. Stir in the herbs and season to taste. Cover and cook the casserole slowly over gentle heat for 45-60 minutes or until the duck is tender. Remove the pieces of duck and strain the casserole liquids into a clean pan. Keep the duck warm in the oven.

4 Boil the ribbon pasta in salted water for 10 minutes. Strain and arrange it on a large ovenproof serv-

ing dish. Toss the pasta in the remaining butter and the cheese and arrange the duck on top. Keep warm.

5 Skim off any fat that may have formed from the top of the casserole juices. Mix the cornstarch and $\frac{1}{4}$ cup of warm water to a paste.

6 Heat the juices gently and stir in the cornstarch paste. Continue to stir over gentle heat until you have a smooth, thick gravy. Pour some of the gravy over the duck and pasta and serve the rest in a gravy boat. Return the duck and pasta to the oven for 5 minutes to allow the gravy to soak through the pasta.

7 Serve with a crisp green salad and a green vegetable of your choice.

Serves 8

Duck Italian-style is cooked in wine with fresh celery, and then served on a bed of ribbon macaroni for a tasty meal

Pineapple Cream

1 cup milk
1 teaspoon vanilla extract
$\frac{1}{4}$ cup all-purpose flour
$\frac{1}{2}$ cup confectioners' sugar
3 egg yolks
2 tablespoons unflavored gelatin
2 tablespoons cherry-flavored liqueur
$\frac{1}{3}$ cup canned chopped pineapple
1 cup heavy cream, whipped

For the Decoration:
pineapple pieces
glacé cherries
angelica

1 In a small saucepan, gently heat the milk and vanilla to just below boiling point. In a bowl, mix the flour and sugar and beat in the egg yolks until throughly blended. Pour the milk gradually into the flour mixture, stirring constantly until smooth.

2 Soften the gelatin in $\frac{1}{4}$ cup of warm water and stir it into the custard cream. Let cool until lukewarm. Add the liqueur and mix well. Chill until partially set and then fold in the pineapple.

3 Whip the cream until it forms stiff peaks and fold it into the pineapple mixture. Turn the pineapple mixture into a 6-cup mold and chill in the refrigerator until well set.

4 Unmold the cream and decorate with the pineapple, cherries and angelica. Serve at once.

Serves 8

Menu

Melon

★

**Glazed Loin of Pork
with Stuffed Pears**

★

Tivoli Salad

★

Bananas Créole

Glazed Loin of Pork with Stuffed Pears

3-lb. boned and rolled loin of pork
1½ ozs. cream cheese
2 tablespoons sweet pickle, chopped
½ cup chopped walnuts
6 canned pear halves, drained
6 small dill pickles cut into fans

For the Marinade:
2 tablespoons each honey, vinegar and oil
¼ cup orange juice
1 tablespoon soy sauce
1 teaspoon paprika
salt and pepper

1 Weigh the meat and calculate the cooking time, allowing 20 minutes per 1 lb. plus 20 minutes.

2 Combine the marinade ingredients and place in a shallow dish with the pork. Marinate for several hours, turning frequently.

3 Preheat the oven to 400°F. Remove the pork from the marinade and place it in a roasting pan. Bake for the calculated cooking time, reducing the oven temperature after 15 minutes to 375°F. and basting with the marinade for the last 30 minutes. Cool the meat on a rack. Remove the string.

4 Blend the cream cheese, pickle

Bananas Creole are a tropical specialty from the sunny Caribbean, and are flamed in rum with pineapple syrup

and walnuts and divide among the pear halves. Garnish the cold meat with the stuffed pears and the dill pickles.

Serves 6

Tivoli Salad

1 lb. red cabbage, shredded
1 cooked beet, cut into strips
4 branches celery, cut into strips
2 apples, cored and sliced
½ small onion, grated
½ cup wine vinegar
2 tablespoons oil
salt and pepper

1 Combine the vegetables.

2 Mix the remaining ingredients and toss with the salad.

Serves 6

Bananas Créole

¼ cup butter
6 bananas, peeled
3 canned pineapple rings, diced
scant ½ cup confectioners' sugar
3 tablespoons syrup from canned pineapple
⅓ cup raisins, plumped in water
¼ cup rum

1 Melt the butter in a skillet. Add the bananas and sauté them in the butter over medium heat until golden.

2 Add the pineapple and sugar, and cook until the sugar has caramelized.

3 Stir in the pineapple syrup, raisins and rum, heat through and ignite. Serve immediately.

Serves 6

Glazed Loin of Pork with Stuffed Pears is served with a colorful, crisp Tivoli Salad of red cabbage and apple

Menu

Stuffed Artichokes

★

Chicken Dijon

★

French Beans

★

Black Cherry Flan

Stuffed Artichokes

4 globe artichokes
salt
juice ½ lemon
6 crushed peppercorns
2 tablespoons vinegar
1 tablespoon water
2 egg yolks
½ cup butter
2 tablespoons capers
10 anchovy fillets

1 Cut off the artichoke stems and about 1 inch off their tops. Trim the leaves with scissors. Place the artichokes in a pan of salted water with the lemon juice and simmer for 30 minutes until tender. Drain and rinse. Remove the centers from each artichoke and discard the 'choke' of hairs. Replace the artichoke centers upside down.

2 Boil the peppercorns in the vinegar and water in a pan until reduced to half of the volume. Cool. Place the egg yolks in a bowl and stir in the vinegar. Place the bowl over a pan of hot water over low heat and beat until the mixture thickens. Add small pieces of butter, gradually beating into the sauce to form a fairly stiff, creamy mixture. Season to taste.

3 Stir the capers into the sauce. Finely chop 2 of the anchovy fillets and add them to the sauce. Divide the sauce between the artichoke shells, top with the remaining anchovy fillets, and serve immediately.

Serves 4

Tip: Use the sauce in the artichokes as a dip, pulling away the leaves from the outside and dipping their soft bases into the sauce before eating the leaf bases only. The soft heart of the artichoke is a delicacy.

Stuffed Artichokes may take a little time to prepare, but the result is worthwhile for that special occasion dinner

Chicken Dijon

¼ cup butter
4 chicken parts
½ cup dry white wine
bouquet garni
salt and white pepper
2 egg yolks
2 tablespoons sour cream
2 tablespoons French mustard
pinch cayenne pepper

1 Melt the butter in a large pan and fry the chicken parts until browned on all sides. Add the wine, bouquet garni and seasoning. Cover; simmer for 25 minutes.

2 Drain the chicken pieces and place them on a heated serving dish. Discard the bouquet garni. Beat together the egg yolks, sour cream, mustard and cayenne Add to the cooking liquor and heat without boiling until thickened, stirring constantly. Pour over the chicken and serve.

Serves 4

Black Cherry Cake

one 10-inch sponge cake
1 lb. canned black pitted cherries
2 tablespoons currant or
   blackberry jelly
⅔ cup heavy cream, whipped

1 Place the sponge cake on a serving dish. Drain the canned cherries, reserving the juice, and arrange the cherries over the cake.

2 Melt the jelly in a pan with ¼ cup of the fruit juice. Pour it on the cherries. Top with whipped cream and serve.

Serves 4–6

Chicken Dijon — crispy and succulent pieces of chicken are robed in a creamy but piquant mustard sauce

Menu

Mussels with Celery
★
Pot-Roast Cornish Hens
★
Broccoli
★
Rhubarb Wine Mold

Mussels with Celery

3 quarts mussels
3 tablespoons oil
6 tomatoes, peeled and chopped
4 branches celery, finely chopped
salt and pepper
⅔ cup plain yogurt

1 Thoroughly clean the mussels. Cook them in the oil until they open. Place them in a heated serving dish.

2 Add the tomatoes and celery to the pan, season and cook for 5 minutes. Stir in the yogurt, pour the sauce over the mussels, and serve hot.

Serves 6–8

Pot-roast Cornish Hens

¼ cup oil
2 tablespoons butter
2 Cornish hens, about 2 lbs. each
2 large carrots, sliced
2 medium onions, chopped
2 large branches celery, chopped
salt and pepper
4 thin slices bacon
⅔ cup cider
⅔ cup chicken stock
1 tablespoon tomato paste
cornstarch for thickening

1 Preheat the oven to 400°F. Melt the oil and butter in a heavy-based metal casserole. Lightly brown the hens all over; remove from the pan.

Mussels with Celery is a pleasantly different way to serve these versatile shellfish, and makes a fine appetizer

2 Place the chopped vegetables in the pan. Season the hens and place two slices of bacon on each one. Set them in the casserole, cover and roast for about 45 minutes or until the birds are tender.

3 Place the hens on a serving dish and keep warm. Pour the cider, stock and tomato paste into the casserole and cook over medium heat for 15 minutes. Strain the vegetables out, adjust the seasoning and thicken, if required, with a little cornstarch dissolved in water. Serve this gravy in a sauce boat. Garnish the hens with roast chestnuts, potatoes, bacon curls, red currant jelly and bread stuffing.

Serves 6–8

Rhubarb Wine Mold

1 lb. rhubarb
2½ cups water
2 cups sugar
strip lemon peel
2 tablespoons unflavored gelatin
½ cup medium or sweet white wine
⅔ cup heavy cream, whipped

1 Cut the rhubarb in 1-inch pieces and cook them for about 25 minutes in the water with the sugar and lemon peel. Remove the lemon peel and strain, reserving the syrup.

2 Dissolve the gelatin in the syrup and cool. Stir in the wine and rhubarb and chill in a mold until set. Turn out and decorate with whipped cream.

Serves 6

Pot-roast Cornish Hens are easy to make and full of flavor

Menu

Chinese Spring Salad
★
Hawaiian Chicken
★
Rice Pilaf
★
Normandy Tart

Chinese Spring Salad

3 cups noodles
1 cucumber, sliced
2 branches celery, sliced
6 ozs. canned bamboo shoots, sliced
6 ozs. cooked shrimp, peeled and deveined
¼ lb. ham, chopped
¼ lb. canned Chinese mushrooms, sliced
24 whole cooked shrimp to garnish

For the Dressing:
salt and pepper
1 tablespoon soy sauce
1 tablespoon vinegar
2 tablespoons oil

1 Cook the egg noodles in boiling, salted water for about 5 minutes until tender. Drain and rinse in cold water.

2 Mix all the other salad ingredients together in a large bowl and stir in the noodles.

3 Beat the seasoning, soy sauce, vinegar and oil together with a fork, until thoroughly blended. Toss the salad in this dressing, and serve garnished with the whole shrimp.

Serves 6

Tip: Chinese mushrooms are sometimes difficult to obtain, so you can substitute sliced white raw mushrooms. Adding some bean sprouts will give the salad a crisper texture.

Chinese Spring Salad, a crisp textured mixture of egg noodles, bamboo shoots and shrimp, makes a refreshing appetizer

Hawaiian Chicken

one 4-lb. oven-ready roasting chicken
salt and pepper
1 tablespoon oil
1 small pineapple, peeled, cored and sliced
¼ lb. lean bacon slices
few sprigs parsley

For the Stuffing:
1 small or ½ large pineapple, peeled, cored and diced
2 tablespoons chopped cashews
2 tablespoons raisins

1 tablespoon oil
1 tablespoon honey
½ teaspoon ground cinnamon
½ teaspoon ground ginger
salt and pepper

For the Glaze:
1 tablespoon honey
3 tablespoons oil
½ cup pineapple juice
1 teaspoon prepared mustard
1 teaspoon soy sauce
salt and pepper

1 Season the chicken inside and out. Preheat the oven to 375°F. Mix the stuffing ingredients and place inside the chicken. Truss the bird with kitchen string.

2 Place the chicken in a roasting pan and sprinkle with oil. Cover with aluminum foil and roast in the preheated oven for 45 minutes. Blend the glaze ingredients together. Remove the foil and brush the chicken with the glaze. Roast for another 45-50 minutes, basting occasionally with the glaze, until the chicken is cooked and golden brown.

3 Remove the chicken from the pan and keep warm. Remove string. Meanwhile sauté the sliced pineapple in the pan juices until golden. Heat the broiler and halve each slice of bacon. Roll up and broil until cooked and crisp.

4 Serve the chicken on an attractive plate surrounded by the pineapple and bacon rolls and garnished with parsley. Strain the pan juices and serve as a gravy.

Serves 6

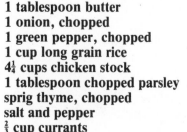

Normandy Tart consists of two puff pastry layers, sandwiched with apple purée and topped with a sugar-icing

Rice Pilaf

1 tablespoon butter
1 onion, chopped
1 green pepper, chopped
1 cup long grain rice
4¼ cups chicken stock
1 tablespoon chopped parsley
sprig thyme, chopped
salt and pepper
⅔ cup currants

1 Heat the butter and sauté the onion and pepper until soft. Add the rice and cook until transparent, but not brown.

2 Add the stock, herbs and seasoning, cover and cook gently for about 20 minutes until the rice is tender and the liquid absorbed. Drain, mix in the currants and serve.

Serves 6

Normandy Tart

1½ lbs. frozen puff pastry, thawed
1 egg yolk
1 tablespoon water
1 egg white
⅔ cup confectioners' sugar, sifted
2 tablespoons sliced almonds, toasted
2 lbs. apples, peeled, cored and sliced
½ cup sugar
1 tablespoon butter

1 Preheat the oven to 375°F. Divide the pastry in two, and roll out each piece to a large circle. Using an 8-inch saucepan lid, cut out two smoothly edged circles. Use the trimmings to make 8 thin strips of pastry, each 4 inches long.

2 Place the pastry circles on two greased baking sheets. Arrange the strips in a star pattern on top of one circle. Prick the pastry all over with a fork. Mix the egg yolk and water and brush the pastry with this glaze.

3 Bake for about 20 minutes until the pastry is crisp and golden brown. Cool.

4 Meanwhile, blend the egg white and confectioners' sugar. Spread this icing evenly over the decorated cooked pastry circle. Sprinkle with the almonds and return the top layer to the oven for a further 2 minutes.

5 Place the apples, sugar and butter in a pan and cook for 10-15 minutes until soft.

6 Spread the bottom pastry layer with the apple purée, cover with the iced layer and serve.

Serves 6

Menu

Mixed Hors d'Oeuvre

★

Pork Chops with Pine Nuts

★

Caraway Sautéed Potatoes

★

Strawberry Shortcake

Minted Cucumber

1 small onion, peeled and thinly sliced
½ large cucumber, thinly sliced
3 tablespoons mint jelly

1 Arrange the onion and cucumber slices overlapping in a shallow dish.

2 Melt the mint jelly and pour it on. Chill before serving.

Makes 6 small servings

Dressed Beets

2 cooked beets, peeled and diced
2 tablespoons oil
1 tablespoon tarragon vinegar
pinch each salt, pepper, sugar and dry mustard
1 tablespoon chopped fresh herbs (parsley, thyme, tarragon, chives)

1 Place the beets in a shallow serving dish.

2 Place the oil, vinegar, seasoning and herbs in a jar and shake vigorously. Pour over the beets and chill before serving.

Makes 6 small servings

Carrot and Coconut Salad

⅔ cup grated carrots
⅓ cup shredded coconut
2 tablespoons raisins
2 tablespoons lemon juice
1 teaspoon ground ginger
⅓ cup mayonnaise

1 Combine all the ingredients and mix well.

2 Chill the salad before serving.

Makes 6 small servings

Eggs with Blue Cheese

4 hard-boiled eggs
2 ozs. blue cheese
1 teaspoon paprika
2 tablespoons light cream
salt and pepper
prepared mustard and watercress
parsley

1 Shell the eggs, cut in half lengthwise and scoop out the yolks into a small bowl. Add the blue cheese and mash together well.

2 Stir in the paprika and cream, season to taste and spoon back into the egg whites.

3 Cover the base of a shallow serving dish with the mustard and watercress and lay the eggs on top, cheese-side upward. Garnish each with a tiny sprig of parsley.

Makes 6–8 small servings

Everglade Shrimp

1 cup plain yogurt
1 tablespoon tomato paste
½ lb. cooked peeled, deveined shrimp

2-3 tablespoons canned sweet corn, drained
watercress

1 Combine the yogurt and tomato paste, then mix in the shrimp and corn.

2 Arrange the watercress in a shallow serving dish and spoon the shrimp mixture on top.

Makes 6 small servings

Pork Chops with Pine Nuts

3 lbs. fresh spinach
6 tablespoons oil
salt and pepper
1 cup raisins
¾ cup pine nuts
2 cloves garlic, crushed
6 pork chops
6 small sprigs parsley

1 Wash the spinach thoroughly and strip the leaves from the stalks. Heat half of the oil in a pan, add the spinach leaves and cook covered over gentle heat for 15 minutes. Add the seasoning, raisins, pine nuts and crushed garlic and cook for a further 15 minutes.

2 Meanwhile, remove the excess fat from the pork chops. Heat the remaining oil in a skillet and fry the pork chops for 15-20 minutes on each side, until cooked through and golden brown.

3 Transfer the cooked chops to a heated serving dish and arrange the spinach and pine nut mixture along one side. Garnish each chop with a sprig of parsley. Serve with Caraway Sautéed Potatoes.

Serves 6

Pork Chops with Pine Nuts is unusual but delicious. The subtle taste of pine nuts goes well with the pork

Caraway Sautéed Potatoes

6 medium-size potatoes
salt and pepper
1 onion
¼ cup shortening
½ teaspoon caraway seeds

1 Peel the potatoes and cook them in boiling salted water for 15-20 minutes, until just tender. Drain the cooked potatoes, rinse them in cold water and drain again. Cut the potatoes into chunky pieces.

2 Peel and slice the onion and separate the slices into rings.

3 Melt the shortening in a skillet and sauté the onion until it is soft, but not golden. Add the potatoes, caraway seeds and seasoning and fry until the potatoes are crisp and brown. Serve immediately with the pork chops.

Serves 6

Tip: For an oriental flavor, this crispy potato dish could be prepared with cumin seeds.

Strawberry Shortcake looks really scrumptious but won't last long — hungry diners will make short work of it!

Strawberry Shortcake

2¼ cups flour
1 tablespoon baking powder
pinch salt
¼ lb. butter
¼ cup sugar
1 egg
⅔ cup milk
1¼ cups heavy cream
1 lb. strawberries, hulled

1 Preheat the oven to 400°F.

2 Sift the flour, baking powder and salt into a bowl and rub in the butter. Stir in the sugar. Beat the egg with the milk, stir into the flour mixture and mix to a soft dough.

3 Divide the dough in half and press each piece into an 8-inch fluted flan ring set on a baking

sheet which has been lined with wax paper. Smooth the mixture down with the fingertips and prick all over with a fork.

4 Bake in the preheated oven for 20-30 minutes, until golden brown. Leave the shortcakes in the rings for ½ hour, then remove the rings and cool completely.

5 Whip the cream until it is thick. Reserve some of the cream for piping and spread the remainder over one layer of shortcake. Reserve a few nice strawberries for the top and arrange the rest over the cream-covered layer.

6 Top with the second shortcake layer, arrange the reserved strawberries on top and decorate with piped cream.

Serves 6

Tip: The strawberries for the filling of this shortcake can, if preferred, be crushed. Although this looks a little less attractive than whole strawberries, you will find that the shortcake is easier to serve.

Customer service: Box 1000, Brattleboro, VT 05301

Text typesetting in Times Roman and Souvenir
by A & B Typesetters, Inc., Concord   NH
Indexes in Helvetica by WordTech Corpor-
ation, Woburn   MA
Covers by Federated Lithographers,
Providence   RI
Printing and binding by Rand McNally,
Versailles   KY
Design and production by Unicorn Produc-
tion Services, Boston   MA
Publisher   Tom Begner
Editorial production: Kathy Shulga, Michael
Michaud
Staff: Erika Petersson, Pam Thompson

© Illustrations Bay Books Pty Ltd., Sydney,
Australia. Reprinted by permission.
© Illustrations from
"Les Cours de la Cuisine A à Z"
"Femmes d'Aujourd'hui"

ISBN 0-914575-12-0

For easy reference, the volumes are numbered
as follows:

1	1-96
2	97-192
3	193-288
4	289-384
5	385-480
6	481-576
7	577-672
8	673-768
9	769-864
10	865-960
11	961-1056
12	1057-1152